Cycling in the
Midlands

Vincent Cassar

D1386475

Editor: Donna Wood
Designer: Phil Barfoot
Copy Editor: Helen Ridge
Proofreader: Judith Forshaw
Picture Researchers: Lesley Grayson (AA)
and Jonathan Bewley (Sustrans)
Image retouching and internal repro:
Sarah Montgomery and James Tims
Cartography provided by the Mapping Services
Department of AA Publishing from data supplied
by Richard Sanders and Sustrans mapping team
Researched and written by: Lindsey Ryle, Melissa
Henry, Julian Hunt, Yvonne Gilligan, Henry Harbord,
Edward Healey, Nicola Jones and Patrick Davis
Supplementary text: Nick Cotton
Production: Lorraine Taylor

Produced by AA Publishing

ISBN: 978-0-7495-7249-5

Published by AA Publishing (a trading name of
AA Media Limited, whose registered office is
Fanum House, Basing View, Basingstoke
RG21 4EA; registered number 06112600).

A04632

Free cycling permits are required on some British
Waterways canal towpaths. Visit www.waterscape.com
or call 0845 671 5530.

The National Cycle Network has been made possible
by the support and co-operation of hundreds of
organisations and thousands of individuals, including:
local authorities and councils, central governments
and their agencies, the National Lottery, landowners,
utility and statutory bodies, countryside and
regeneration bodies, the Landfill Communities Fund,
other voluntary organisations, charitable trusts and
foundations, the cycle trade and industry, corporate
sponsors, community organisations and Sustrans'
supporters. Sustrans would also like to extend thanks
to the thousands of volunteers who generously
contribute their time to looking after their local
sections of the Network.

We have taken all reasonable steps to ensure that
the cycle rides in this book are safe and achievable
by people with a reasonable level of fitness. However,
all outdoor activities involve a degree of risk and the
publishers accept no responsibility for any injuries
caused to readers while following these cycle rides.

The contents of this book are believed correct at the
time of printing. Nevertheless, the publishers cannot
be held responsible for any errors or omissions or for
changes in the details given in this book or for the
consequences of any reliance on the information
provided by the same. This does not affect your
statutory rights.

Printed and bound in Dubai by Oriental Press
theAA.com/shop

Sustrans
2 Cathedral Square
College Green
Bristol BS1 5DD
www.sustrans.org.uk

Sustrans is a Registered Charity in the UK:
Number 326550 (England and Wales)
SC039263 (Scotland).

CONTENTS

Foreword by Dave Gorman   4

Introduction   6

National Cycle Network facts & figures   8

Locator map   9

Cycling with children   10

Hot tips & cool tricks   12

Bike maintenance   13

THE RIDES

1 Worcester to Pershore   14

2 Worcester to Droitwich   18

3 Hampton Loade to Bewdley   22

4 Telford to Ironbridge Gorge   26

5 Gobowen to Colemere Country Park   30

6 Stratford Greenway   34

7 Redditch to Stratford-upon-Avon   38

8 Plantsbrook Valley   42

9 The Lias Line Cycleway   46

10 Around Market Bosworth   50

11 Brampton Valley Way   54

12 Rutland Water Circuit   58

13 Gartree Ride   62

14 Great Central Way   66

15 Lichfield City to Burton upon Trent 70

16 Mountsorrel to Loughborough & Shepshed 74

17 Ashby Woulds Heritage Trail   78

18 Derby Canal Path & The Cloud Trail   82

19 Nutbrook Trail   86

20 Nottingham's Big Track   90

21 Silver Hill & Five Pits Trail   94

22 The Manifold Trail – Staffordshire   98

23 Tissington & High Peak Trails   102

24 Around Grantham   107

25 Around Southwell   110

26 Lincoln to Harby Circuit   114

27 The Water Rail Way   118

28 Woodhall Spa   122

Next steps   126

Join Sustrans   127

Acknowledgements   128

A bike meant I cou the world on my o

Foreword by **Dave Gorman,** writer and comedian

I have strong memories of learning to ride a bike. That's mainly because my parents didn't believe in stabilizers. They wanted me to learn quickly and were prepared to put up with the odd bloody knee if that's what it took (and that *is* what it took).

When I was growing up a bike was essential. A bike gave me my first taste of independence. A bike meant I could start to head off and explore the world on my own terms. At the time I didn't imagine that all these years later I'd still be cycling. I thought that as I grew up my bike would be left behind, consigned to the past, dismissed – like computer games and cartoons – as the stuff of childhood. How wrong can a Nintendo Wii-owning, Simpsons-watching cyclist be?

The thing is, when I was a kid, I don't think I knew any adult cyclists. Adults drove cars. Children rode bikes. That's how it was and that's how I imagined it would always be. But after a few years of life as a motorist, I found that the adult me started flirting with cycling once more. It started out with very occasional fair-weather jaunts, but over the years the infatuation grew until, eventually, I accepted the obvious truth and gave in to it completely. I got rid of my car.

If further proof was needed that I've been well and truly smitten, I recently completed a ride of nearly 1,600 miles, travelling from the southernmost point of the British mainland to the easternmost, westernmost and then northernmost points. Just to make things

> *"I do reckon that most of us could benefit from cycling more than we already do"*

d ... explore wn terms

trickier for myself, I also did a stage show every night along the way while I was at it... but that's another story.

Of course, I don't expect everyone to be as bitten by the bug as I am. I don't evangelize about giving up the car because I know my circumstances – I'm a child-free adult living two minutes' walk away from great shops in a city well served by public transport – aren't shared by most, but I do reckon that most of us could benefit from cycling more than we already do.

Every cyclist's motivation is different: for some it's to do with their health; for others it's the environment; for me, it's mainly to do with convenience. And fun. I sometimes forget that. It's bloody good fun.

Whatever motivates you and however you cycle – whether you just do the five-mile trip into work every now and then or you spend every weekend burning up the miles in your lycra – this guide should have something to offer you. My hope is that it will help motivate you to do more. Maybe you'll only use parts of the routes to help you get from A to B. Maybe you'll follow them all faithfully from start to finish. Use them your way. Make them your own. For me, cycling more started with simply knowing that more was possible. In many ways, I have Sustrans to thank for that.

"Every cyclist's motivation is different: for some it's to do with their health; for others it's the environment..."

INTRODUCTION

Within the Midlands and the Heart of England lie some of the UK's most fascinating counties, with beautiful rolling countryside bordering fertile fens, historic houses and castles, ancient market towns and chocolate-box villages. This guide covers Derbyshire, Herefordshire, Leicestershire, Lincolnshire, Nottinghamshire, Rutland, Shropshire, Staffordshire, Warwickshire and Worcestershire.

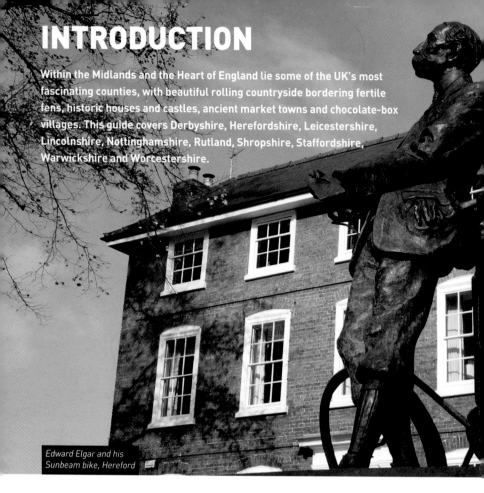

Edward Elgar and his Sunbeam bike, Hereford

Travelling the country lanes, byways, canal towpaths and disused railway tracks of the Midlands region offers opportunities for cyclists of all ages and abilities. You'll find a broad patchwork of unspoilt countryside, dotted with old market towns and a unique industrial heritage, as well as progressive, multicultural cities.

The region has many famous historical and cultural landmarks on or near the National Cycle Network, including the site of the Battle of Bosworth (Leicestershire), Lincoln Cathedral, one of the most superb Gothic buildings in Europe, Sherwood Forest of Robin Hood fame, and the Ironbridge Gorge near Telford, now a UNESCO World Heritage Site. Most of the routes in this book either follow traffic-free tracks, such as the Nutbrook Trail

and Brampton Valley Way, or use quiet country lanes, like the Stratford Greenway. Several routes will take you through the major connurbations of Birmingham, Leicester, Worcester and Nottingham, as well as lively and historic towns, such as Stratford and Rugby. You can also cycle around Shakespeare country, and visit the Bard's birthplace in Stratford-upon-Avon.

Some of the areas featured in this guide were replete with industry until the last century but then fell into decline. Since then, a great deal of time, money and energy has been invested in a programme of regeneration, with former scars on the landscape – coal mines and gravel pits – transformed into beautiful lakes and parks. Derbyshire's Five Pits Trail, for example, follows the track beds of the former

'Lincoln Red Cattle' by Sally Matthews

Ironbridge town and River Severn

Safe and easy-going canalside cycling

colliery railways, which, together with the local footpaths, provide a network of varied and enchanting cycle rides through countryside abundant with wildlife.

The National Forest is one of Britain's boldest environmental projects: the creation of a new forest for the nation, across 200 square miles (518 sq km) and embracing parts of Leicestershire, Staffordshire and Derbyshire. Within its boundary are miles of rolling farmland and a former coalfield. Forest towns and villages include Burton-upon-Trent, Coalville, Swadlincote, and historic Ashby-de-la-Zouch. In just over ten years, more than seven million trees have been planted in this area and the woodland cover has almost trebled. The National Forest has a network of quiet country lanes and cycling trails, among

them the Ashby Woulds Heritage Trail, going from Moira to Measham. It's one of many routes that allow you to explore Derbyshire's stunning rolling hills, rugged peaks, canal towpaths and gentle greenways.

Shropshire, Herefordshire and Worcestershire are perhaps the quietest corners of the region to explore. Cycling around these counties can be a relaxing and rewarding pastime – there are only a few hills, combined with empty lanes and country roads, the gradients are easy and the views amazing.

It couldn't be easier to explore the Midlands of England on two wheels. These routes are free to use and open to all, making them a great way for you and your family to stay fit and healthy, while enjoying the countryside and enjoying a breath of fresh air.

NATIONAL CYCLE NETWORK FACTS & FIGURES

Most of the routes featured here are part of the National Cycle Network. The aim of this book is to enable you to sample some of the highlights of the region on two wheels, but the rides given here are really just a taster, as there are more than 13,000 miles of Network throughout the UK to explore. More than three-quarters of us live within just two miles of one of the routes.

Over one million journeys a day are made on the National Cycle Network; for special trips like fun days out and holiday bike rides, but also the necessary everyday trips; taking people to school, to work, to the shops, to visit each other and to seek out green spaces. Half of these journeys are made on foot and half by bike, with urban traffic-free sections of the Network seeing the most usage.

The National Cycle Network is host to one of the UK's biggest collections of public art. Sculptures, benches, water fountains, viewing points and award-winning bridges enhance its pathways, making Sustrans one of the most prolific commissioners of public art in the UK.

The Network came into being following the award of the first-ever grant from the lottery, through the Millennium Commission, in 1995. Funding for the Network also came from bike retailers and manufacturers through the Bike Hub, as well as local authorities and councils UK-wide, and Sustrans' many supporters. Over 2,500 volunteer Rangers give their time to Sustrans to assist in the maintenance of the National Cycle Network by adopting sections of route in communities throughout the UK. They remove glass and litter, cut back vegetation and try to ensure routes are well signed.

Developing and maintaining the National Cycle Network is just one of the ways in which Sustrans pursues its vision of a world in which people can choose to travel in ways that benefit their health and the environment.

We hope that you enjoy using this book to explore the paths and cycleways of the National Cycle Network and we would like to thank the many hundreds of organisations who have worked with Sustrans to develop the walking and cycling routes, including every local authority and council in the UK.

MAP LEGEND

- - - -	Traffic Free/On Road route	O	Ride Start or Finish Point	- - - -	National Cycle Network (Traffic Free)

National Cycle Network (On Road)

PH	AA recommended pub		Farm or animal centre		Theme park
	Abbey, cathedral or priory		Garden	i	Tourist Information Centre
	Abbey, cathedral or priory in ruins		Hill-fort		Viewpoint
	Aquarium		Historic house	V	Visitor or heritage centre
	Aqueduct or viaduct		Industrial attraction		World Heritage Site (UNESCO)
	Arboretum		Marina		Zoo or wildlife collection
X	Battle site		Monument		AA golf course
RSPB	Bird Reserve (RSPB)	M	Museum or gallery		Stadium
	Cadw (Welsh Heritage) site		National Nature Reserve: England, Scotland, Wales		Indoor Arena
A	Campsite		Local nature reserve		Tennis
	Caravan site		National Trust property		Horse racing
A	Caravan & campsite		National Trust for Scotland property		Rugby Union
X	Castle		Picnic site		Football
	Cave		Roman remains		Athletics
	Country park		Steam railway		Motorsports
	English Heritage site				County cricket

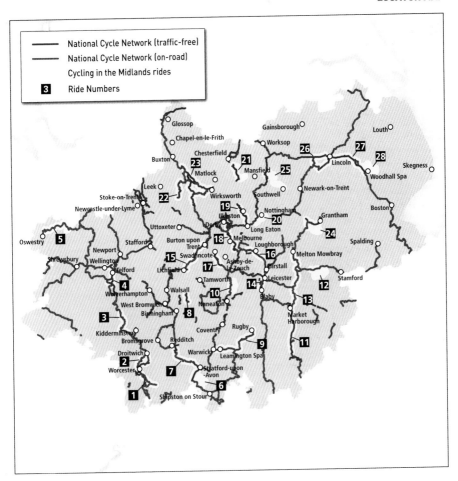

KEY TO LOCATOR MAP

1 Worcester to Pershore
2 Worcester to Droitwich
3 Hampton Loade to Bewdley
4 Telford to Ironbridge Gorge
5 Gobowen to Colemere Country Park
6 Stratford Greenway
7 Redditch to Stratford-upon-Avon
8 Plantsbrook Valley
9 The Lias Line Cycleway
10 Around Market Bosworth
11 Brampton Valley Way
12 Rutland Water Circuit
13 Gartree Ride
14 Great Central Way
15 Lichfield City to Burton upon Trent
16 Mountsorrel to Loughborough & Shepshed
17 Ashby Woulds Heritage Trail
18 Derby Canal Path & The Cloud Trail
19 Nutbrook Trail
20 Nottingham's Big Track
21 Silver Hill & Five Pits Trail
22 The Manifold Trail – Staffordshire
23 Tissington & High Peak Trails
24 Around Grantham
25 Around Southwell
26 Lincoln to Harby Circuit
27 The Water Rail Way
28 Woodhall Spa

CYCLING WITH CHILDREN

Kids love bikes and love to ride. Cycling helps them to grow up fit, healthy and independent, and introduces them to the wider world and the adventure it holds.

TOP TIPS FOR FAMILY BIKE RIDES:

- Take along snacks, drinks and treats to keep their energy and spirit levels up.
- Don't be too ambitious. It's much better that everyone wants to go out again, than all coming home exhausted, tearful and permanently put off cycling.
- Plan your trip around interesting stops and sights along the way. Don't make journey times any longer than children are happy to sit and play at home.
- Even on a fine day, take extra clothes and waterproofs – just in case. Check that trousers and laces can't get caught in the chain when pedalling along.
- Wrap up toddlers. When a young child is on the back of a bike, they won't be generating heat like the person doing all the pedalling!
- Be careful not to pinch their skin when putting their helmet on. It's easily done and often ends in tears. Just place your forefinger between the clip and the chin.
- Ride in a line with the children in the middle of the adults. If there's only one of you, the adult should be at the rear, keeping an eye on all the children in front. Take special care at road junctions.
- Check that children's bikes are ready to ride. Do the brakes and gears work? Is the saddle the right height? Are the tyres pumped up?
- Carry some sticking plasters and antiseptic wipes – kids are far more likely to fall off and graze arms, hands or knees.
- Take a camera to record the trip – memories are made of this.

TRANSPORTING YOUNG CHILDREN ON TWO WHEELS

It's now easier than ever for you to ride your bike with young children.

- **Child seats:** *6 months to five years (one child).* Once a baby can support its own head (usually at 6–12 months) they can be carried in a child seat. Seats are fitted mainly to the rear of the bike.
- **Trailers:** babies to five years *(up to two children).* Young babies can be strapped into their car seat and carried in a trailer, and older children can be strapped in and protected from the wind and rain.
- **Tag-along trailer bikes:** *approx four to nine years.* Tag-alongs (the back half of a child's bike attached to the back of an adult one) allow a child to be towed while they either add some of their own pedal power or just freewheel and enjoy the ride.
- **Tow bar:** *approx four to eight years.* A tow bar converts a standard child's bike to a trailer bike by lifting their front wheel from the ground to prevent them from steering, while enabling them to pedal independently. When you reach a safe place, the tow bar can be detached and the child's bike freed.

TEACHING YOUR CHILD TO RIDE

There are lots of ways for children to develop and gain cycling confidence before they head out on their own.

- **Tricycles or trikes:** available for children from ten months to five years old. They have pedals so kids have all the fun of getting around under their own steam.
- **Balance bikes:** are like normal bikes but without the pedals. This means children learn to balance, steer and gain confidence on two wheels while being able to place their feet firmly and safely on the ground.

- **Training wheels:** stabilisers give support to the rear of the bike and are the easiest way to learn to ride but potentially the slowest.

BUYING THE RIGHT BIKE FOR YOUR CHILD

Every child develops differently and they may be ready to learn to ride between the ages of three and seven. When children do progress to their own bike, emphasising the fun aspect will help them take the tumbles in their stride. Encouragement and praise are important to help them persevere.

Children's bikes generally fall into age categories based on the average size of a child of a specific age. There are no hard and fast rules, as long as your child isn't stretched and can reach the brakes safely and change gear easily. It's important to buy your child a bike that fits them rather than one they can grow into. Ask your local bike shop for advice and take your child along to try out different makes and sizes.

To find a specialist cycle retailer near you visit www.thecyclingexperts.co.uk

HOT TIPS & COOL TRICKS...

WHAT TO WEAR

For most of the rides featured in this book you do not need any special clothing or footwear. Shoes that are suitable for walking are also fine for cycling. Looser-fitting trousers allow your legs to move more freely, while tops with zips let you regulate your temperature. In cold weather, take gloves and a warm hat; it's also a good idea to pack a waterproof. If you are likely to be out at dusk, take a bright reflective top. If you start to cycle regularly, you may want to invest in some specialist equipment for longer rides, especially padded shorts and gloves.

WHAT TO TAKE

For a short ride, the minimum you will need is a pump and a small tool bag with a puncture repair kit, just in case. However, it is worth considering the following: water bottle, spare inner tube, 'multi-tool' (available from cycle shops), lock, money, sunglasses, lightweight waterproof (some pack down as small as a tennis ball), energy bars, map, camera and a spare top in case it cools down or to keep you warm when you stop for refreshments.

HOW TO TAKE IT

Rucksacks are fine for light loads but can make your back hot and sweaty. For heavier loads and for longer or more regular journeys, you are better off with panniers that attach to a bike rack.

BIKE ACCESSORIES

You may also want to invest in a helmet. A helmet will not prevent accidents from happening but can provide protection if you do fall off your bike. They are particularly recommended for young children. Ultimately, wearing a helmet is a question of individual choice and parents need to make that choice for their children.

A bell is a must for considerate cyclists. A friendly tinkle warns that you are approaching, but never assume others can hear you.

LOCKING YOUR BIKE

Unless you are sitting right next to your bike when you stop for refreshments, it is worth locking it, preferably to something immovable like a post, fence or railings (or a bike stand, of course). If nothing else, lock it to a companion's bike. Bike theft is more common in towns and cities, and if you regularly leave your bike on the streets, it is important to invest in a good-quality lock and to lock and leave your bike in a busy, well-lit location.

GETTING TO THE START OF A RIDE

The best rides are often those that you can do right from your doorstep, maximizing time on your bike and reducing travelling time. If you need to travel to the start of the ride, have you thought about catching a train?

FINDING OUT MORE – WWW.SUSTRANS.ORG.UK

Use the Sustrans website to find out where you can cycle to from home or while you are away on holiday, and browse through a whole host of other useful information. Visit www.sustrans.org.uk

MAKING THE MOST OF YOUR BIKE

Making a few simple adjustments to your bike will make your ride more enjoyable and comfortable:

- **Saddle height:** raise or lower it so that you have good contact with your pedals (to make the most of your leg power) and so that you can always put a reassuring foot on the ground.
- **Saddle position:** getting the saddle in the right place will help you get the most from your pedal power without straining your body.
- **Handlebars:** well-positioned handlebars are crucial for your comfort and important for control of your steering and brakes.

...BIKE MAINTENANCE

Like any machine, a bike will work better and last longer if you care for it properly. Get in the habit of checking your bike regularly – simple checks and maintenance can help you have hassle-free riding and avoid repairs.

- **Tools:** there are specialist tools for specific tasks, but all you need to get started are: a pump, an old toothbrush, lubricants and grease, cleaning rags, a puncture repair kit, tyre levers, allen keys, screwdrivers and spanners.

REGULAR CHECKS

- **Every week:** Check tyres, brakes, lights, handlebars and seat are in good order and tightly secured.
- **Every month:** Wipe clean and lubricate chain with chain oil.
  Wipe the dirt from wheels.
  Check tread on tyres.
  Check brake pads.
  Check gear and brake cables and make sure that gears are changing smoothly.
- **Every year:** Take your bike to an experienced mechanic for a thorough service.
- **Tip:** If in doubt, leave it to the professionals. Bike mechanics are much more affordable than car mechanics, and some will even collect the bike from your home and return it to you when all the work is done.

FIXING A PUNCTURE

Punctures don't happen often and are easy to fix yourself. If you don't fancy repairing a puncture on your journey, carry a spare inner tube and a pump so you can change the tube, then fix the puncture when you get home. If you don't mind repairing punctures when they happen, make sure you carry your repair kit and pump with you at all times. All puncture repair kits have full instructions with easy-to-follow pictures.

Alternatively, if you don't want to get your hands dirty, just visit your local bike shop and they will fix the puncture for you.

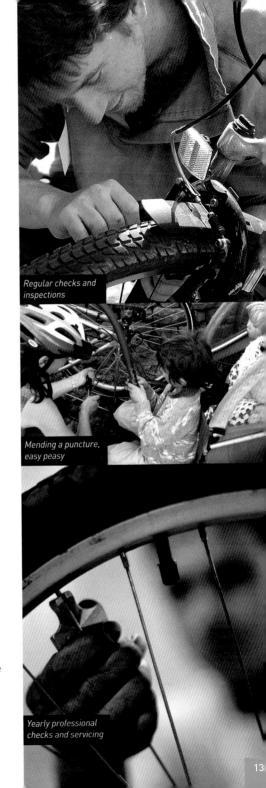

Regular checks and inspections

Mending a puncture, easy peasy

Yearly professional checks and servicing

WORCESTER TO PERSHORE

This attractive route links Worcester Cathedral to Pershore Abbey via a mixture of back streets, country lanes and off-road cyclepaths.

Worcester is the site of the final battle of the English Civil War in 1651, and there is an exhibition dedicated to the war in the same building that King Charles II used to plan his campaign. The Commandery, also known as St Wulfstan's Hospital, is a fascinating site, which has been a monastic hospital and a college for blind boys in the past. The nearby Fort Royal Park has been hailed as one of the ten best urban parks in England.

Pershore is an unspoilt, picturesque market town, famed for its elegant Georgian architecture and magnificent abbey. Surrounded by beautiful countryside and charming villages, it is a haven for cyclists and ramblers. Many of the buildings along Bridge Street and Broad Street are listed, and Pershore has been designated as a town of major architectural importance. In summer, the tower of the abbey is often open and it is well worth climbing to the top for a stunning view of the Vale and Bredon Hill.

ROUTE INFORMATION

Regional Route: 44
Start: Fountain, South Quay, Worcester.
Finish: Pershore Abbey.
Distance: 10 miles (16km).
Grade: Easy.
Surface: Tarmac roads, tracks, country lanes.
Hills: Mainly flat, although there is a steep hill coming into Pershore Abbey.

King Charles House, Worcester

YOUNG & INEXPERIENCED CYCLISTS

Mostly quiet lanes with some traffic-free sections, although there are a few busier roads on the way out of Worcester.

REFRESHMENTS

- Lots of choice in Worcester.
- Lots of choice in Pershore, including The Brandy Cask pub.

THINGS TO SEE & DO

- **Worcester Cathedral:** overlooking the River Severn; built between 1084 and 1504; famous for its Norman crypt and unique chapter house; 01905 732900; www.worcestercathedral.co.uk
- **The Commandery:** glorious Grade I listed site dating back to the 12th century, with displays covering its own history and the English Civil War; 01905 361821; www.worcestercitymuseums.org.uk
- **Guildhall:** superb Queen Anne building with exceptional period interior decoration; 01905 723471; www.worcester.gov.uk
- **Fort Royal Park:** wonderful hilltop views towards Worcester Cathedral and the Commandery; rose garden, extensive flowerbeds and an earthwork, which is Fort Royal itself; www.worcester.gov.uk

Worcester Cathedral and River Severn

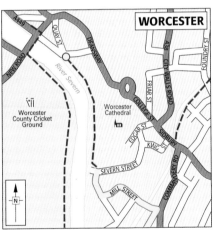

- **The Greyfriars:** 15th-century merchant's house with panelled interior full of interesting textiles and furnishings; beautiful walled garden; 01905 23571; www.nationaltrust.org.uk
- **Pershore Abbey:** founded in AD 689; one of the finest examples of Norman and Early English architecture in the country; 01386 552071; www.pershoreabbey.org.uk
- **Croome Landscape Park:** on National Route 45, south of this ride; 'Capability' Brown's first complete park; features a lakeside garden

with islands, bridges and grotto, wonderful park buildings and miles of walks through lakeland gardens, shrubbery and open parkland; 01905 371006; www.nationaltrust.org.uk

TRAIN STATIONS
Worcester Foregate Street; Worcester Shrub Hill; Pershore.

BIKE HIRE
- **Peddlers, Worcester:** 01905 24238

FURTHER INFORMATION
- To view or print National Cycle Network routes, visit www.sustrans.org.uk
- Maps for this area are available to buy from www.sustransshop.co.uk
- **Worcester Tourist Information:** 01905 726311; www.visitworcester.com
- **Pershore Tourist Information:** 01386 556591; www.visitpershore.co.uk

ROUTE DESCRIPTION
Follow the Regional Route 44 signs left along South Quay in Worcester, with the River Severn to your right. It becomes a traffic-free route for a short spell as you pass Worcester Cathedral. You join the road at Severn Street and follow

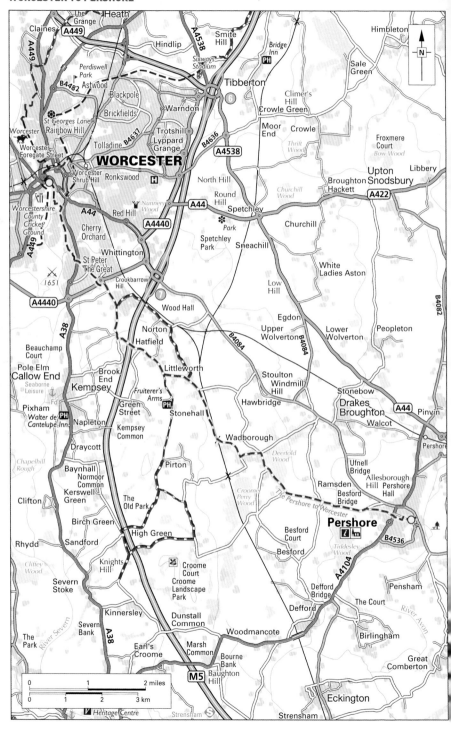

Pershore Abbey

this until you get to the end of St Mark's Close. At the end is Barneshall Avenue, where you get back on-road. Take care as you cross the A38 Bath Road and find yourself on Norton Road. This road ends with a traffic-free lane for about 500m (549 yards) until it rejoins Norton Road. Take the traffic-free route down Broomhall Green over the roundabout. You rejoin Norton Road. Take care on this section, as there can be some heavy traffic.

When you come up to the roundabout just before St Peter's Garden Centre, the route splits in two. Take the southern (straight on) route as it is the more attractive of the two (the other serves Norton). You now find yourself in Broomhall. Go over the M5 into Hatfield. The alternative route joins this just

before you get to Abbotswood. Take care on the level crossing into Wadborough. Go past Deerfold Wood on your left and over Besford Bridge on your way into Pershore. There is a steep hill down Holloway on your way to Pershore Abbey.

NEARBY CYCLE ROUTES

National Route 45 (South) connects Worcester to Kinnersley and uses part of this Pershore route. This lovely, quiet lane provides a direct link into the National Trust's Croome Landscape Park.

Route 45 (North) takes you from Worcester and Offerton Farm on the Worcester & Birmingham Canal and on to Droitwich Spa on country roads (see page 18).

WORCESTER TO DROITWICH

Two popular routes between Worcester and Droitwich are described here. Ride them individually, or make a day of it and combine the two to make a loop. National Cycle Network Route 45 links Droitwich and Worcester on the eastern side of the two towns, and follows a combination of quiet lanes and the towpath of the Worcester & Birmingham Canal. The route will eventually extend from Salisbury in Wiltshire to Chester in Cheshire. Route 46 currently links Worcester and Droitwich on the western side. This is an on-road route that follows a similar line to the Droitwich Canal for much of the way. It enters Worcester via the racecourse (signed diversion in place on race days).

The 14th-century tower of Worcester Cathedral dominates the city by the banks of the River Severn. Among Worcester's many other attractive old buildings are the 15th-century Commandery, once almshouses for the aged and the poor and now a visitor centre. (This is right next to Route 45.)

In Droitwich, visitors to the spa baths can float in the natural spring waters pumped up from the bed of rock salt located 200ft under the town.

ROUTE INFORMATION

National Routes: 46, 45
Start: Diglis Bridge, Worcester.
Finish: Droitwich train station.

Distance: Both routes are just under 10 miles (16km).
Grade: Easy to moderate.
Surface: Both routes have good all-weather surfaces.
Hills: Mainly flat. Short hills in the middle of both routes.

YOUNG & INEXPERIENCED CYCLISTS

Crossing of some fairly busy roads is required at both ends of each route, but this can easily be done on foot if young children find it tricky to ride across.

REFRESHMENTS

• Lots of choice in Worcester, including the Cavalier Tavern, right on the canal towpath, the

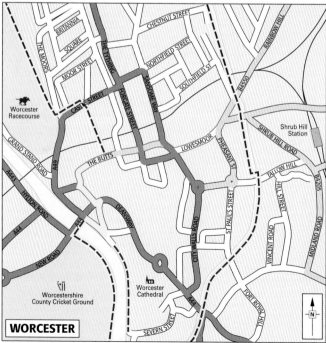

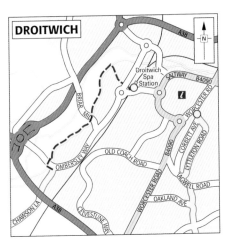

*Worcester Cathedral
on the River Severn*

Pump House Environmental Centre and the Diglis House Hotel, where you can enjoy a drink or a meal on the banks of the River Severn.
- The **Mug House Inn, Bewdley**
- Choices in Droitwich.

THINGS TO SEE & DO
Worcester:
- **Guildhall**: housed in a beautiful building which dates back to 1721; 01905 722033
- **Cathedral**: 01905 732900; www.worcestercathedral.co.uk
- **Worcester Porcelain Museum**: ceramic collections, archives and records of factory production; 01905 21247; www.worcesterporcelainmuseum.org
- **Droitwich Spa**: attractive town centre dotted with medieval churches and half-timbered buildings.

TRAIN STATIONS
Worcester Foregate Street; Worcester Shrub Hill; Droitwich Spa.

BIKE HIRE
- **Peddlers, Worcester**: 01905 24238
- **Midland Cycle Hire**: free cycle delivery

across Worcestershire; 01562 711144; www.midlandcyclehire.co.uk

FURTHER INFORMATION
- To view or print National Cycle Network routes, visit www.sustrans.org.uk
- Maps for this area are available to buy from www.sustransshop.co.uk
- **Worcester Tourist Information**: 01905 726311; www.visitworcester.com
- **Droitwich Spa Tourist Information**: 01905 774312
- To make the route circular, use *Droitwich to Worcester Cycle Routes Map* from Worcestershire Hub; 01905 765 765; www.whub.org.uk

ROUTE DESCRIPTION
Both routes start at the traffic-free Diglis Bridge, the centrepiece of the Lottery-funded project delivered by a partnership between Sustrans, Worcestershire County Council and Worcester City Council.
National Route 46: From Diglis Bridge, follow the riverside path north, with the river on your right (you will pass Diglis Weir on your right), cross New Road (via a pair of toucan crossings) and continue following the river until

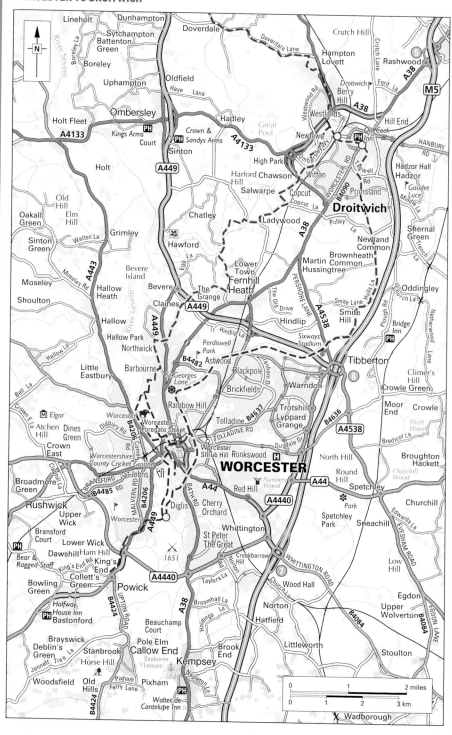

you reach Sabrina Bridge (also traffic-free). Cross the river here and then turn left to enter Pitchcroft Racecourse. (On race days, turn right and skirt around the southern end of the racecourse to find the signed alternative route that begins at the junction of Castle Street and The Moors.) Pass through the grandstand area, following the river (now on your left) all the way to the northern end of the racecourse. Enter Waterworks Road and follow NCN46 signs. At the Pump House Environmental Centre (refreshments available here), turn left onto the cyclepath across the park. (The race-day diversion route rejoins here.)

Continue to follow NCN 46 signs, taking care at the junction in Claines (near a church) and also taking care roughly a third of a mile after turning left into Dilmore Lane; there can be gravel on a tight bend at the bottom of a steep descent. On entering Droitwich, follow the signed route until you meet the bank of the canal; at the footbridge bear right to follow Route 45 to the station.

National Route 45: From Diglis Bridge, head north with the river on your left (passing Diglis Lock on your left) and follow a quiet access road before joining the riverside path. Keep following the river north until you meet the junction between the river and the Worcester & Birmingham Canal. Leave the river here and follow the canal (signposted for Droitwich). Cross over two small swing bridges and then, to the rear of the Anchor Inn, join Route 45, following the towpath for roughly 5 miles (8km) to the outskirts of the city. Leave the towpath as directed by the signs and join Offerton Lane, then follow the signed route on quiet roads. On entering the stopped-off road on the outskirts of Droitwich, take care on the steep descent before entering Droitwich.

NEARBY CYCLE ROUTES

National Routes 45 and Regional Route 44 head south from Worcester towards Tewkesbury and Pershore respectively. Route 45 also heads north from Droitwich to Stourport, Bridgnorth and Telford.

Bridge over Droitwich Canal in Vines Park

HAMPTON LOADE TO BEWDLEY

Cyclists can now enjoy some of Shropshire's most spectacular scenery by travelling the Mercian Way. Running from Hampton Loade to the ancient Wyre Forest near Bewdley, the route not only covers quiet rural lanes, it includes miles of off-road tracks that take the cyclist past unspoilt riversides, woods and meadows. The Highley section offers a unique opportunity to cycle alongside the vintage steam trains of the Severn Valley Railway in a safe, family-friendly, traffic-free environment.

There are plenty of country pubs and village shops providing food and drink along the way, and plenty of family-friendly attractions. In addition, there's one of the oldest arboretums in the country – Arley, set up nearly 200 years ago. You can take a river crossing via the historic Hampton Loade Ferry or ride through the award-winning Severn Valley Country Park at Alveley.

The ride ends at Bewdley, an attractive town that has been described as the most perfect small Georgian town in Worcestershire. Its strongly defined character is based upon a well-related collection of fine historic buildings and a series of landmark set pieces. These include Thomas Telford's Bridge, constructed in 1798, the imposing St Anne's Church at the head of Load Street and the river frontage and former quayside.

ROUTE INFORMATION

National Route: 45
Start: Hampton Loade train station (steam railway).
Finish: Bewdley town centre.
Distance: 12.5 miles (20km).
Grade: Moderate.

Steam train along the Mercian Way

Surface: Tarmac and fine gravel paths.
Hills: Mostly flat, but Wyre Forest has some steep gradients.

YOUNG & INEXPERIENCED CYCLISTS

The early section along the railway line is traffic-free. The route becomes quite hilly in the Wyre Forest. Take care on the B4194 near Buttonoak.

REFRESHMENTS

- River & Rail Country Inn, Hampton Loade.
- Cafe and picnic area in Severn Valley Country Park.
- Lots of choice in Bewdley.

THINGS TO SEE & DO

- Dudmaston Estate: late 17th-century mansion with art collections, lakes, woodland and country walks; 01746 780866; www.nationaltrust.org.uk
- Hampton Loade Ferry: unique current-operated passenger ferry linking the villages of Hampton Loade and Hampton, separated by the River Severn; 07805 865053; www.hamptonloadeferry.co.uk

- **Severn Valley Country Park:** award-winning 126-acre country park with an extensive network of footpaths and bridleways through wetlands, reed beds, woodland and fields full of wildflowers; 01743 255061; www.shropshire.gov.uk
- **Severn Valley Railway:** steam trains that travel from Bridgnorth to Kidderminster and back; 01299 403816; www.svr.co.uk
- **Engine House, Highley:** visitor and education centre with steam locomotives; restaurant with excellent views across the railway and the Severn Valley, a picnic area and a giftshop; 01746 862387; www.svr.co.uk
- **Arley Arboretum:** more than 300 species of trees in formal and informal gardens, including many rare and spectacular domestic and exotic trees; 01299 861368; www.arley-arboretum.org.uk
- **Wyre Forest:** one of the largest ancient lowland coppice oak woodlands in England; noted for its breeding birds and wildlife, including buzzards, ravens, polecats and minks; 01299 266929; www.naturalengland.org.uk

Arley station on the Severn Valley Railway

- **Bewdley Museum:** set in historic Shambles (originally a street of butchers' shops), with fascinating displays on the trades and crafts of the Wyre Forest area; 01562 732928; www.wyreforestdc.gov.uk

TRAIN STATIONS
Kidderminster.

Wyre Forest

《Forest walks·

Severnside South on the River Severn

BIKE HIRE

None locally.

FURTHER INFORMATION

- To view or print National Cycle Network routes, visit www.sustrans.org.uk
- Maps for this area are available to buy from www.sustransshop.co.uk
- Bridgnorth Tourist Information: 01746 763257; www.shropshiretourism.co.uk
- Bewdley Tourist Information: 01299 404740; www.wychavon.gov.uk
- Mercian Way: www.ncr45mercianway.co.uk

ROUTE DESCRIPTION

From Hampton Loade train station, pick up the cyclepath that starts near the entrance to the station car park and simply follow it south.

On this part of the ride, you are sandwiched between the railway track on one side and the River Severn on the other. There is an opportunity here to take in Highley's Sculpture & History Trails, which are adorned with sculptures, bronzes and ceramics showing the history of Highley from the time of the Domesday Book to the present day.

The ride runs parallel to the track from here until it gets to Country Park Halt station. You then turn left across the River Severn Bridge towards Severn Valley Country Park. The route goes through Nash End and down through Upper Arley. After a short while, you go over the River Severn and over the railway track just past Arley station. You pass through Pound Green and when you reach Buttonoak, turn right. Take care here, for after about 600m (660 yards) or so you are on the B4194. Take the first left onto the traffic-free route through the Wyre Forest. It's worth pointing out that the greenway through the Wyre Forest is probably not suitable for the skinniest road tyres.

You eventually come out of the forest at Dry Mill Lane. Follow the signs to take you to Bewdley town centre.

NEARBY CYCLE ROUTES

The Mercian Way (National Route 45) carries on south to Stourport-on-Severn. To the north, the route continues from Hampton Loade to join a bridleway around Chelmarsh Reservoir and busier roads towards Bridgnorth. Further north, the route is also open between Ironbridge and Whitchurch. Open sections of the route are mapped on three route guides available from the Shropshire County Council website (www.shropshire.gov.uk).

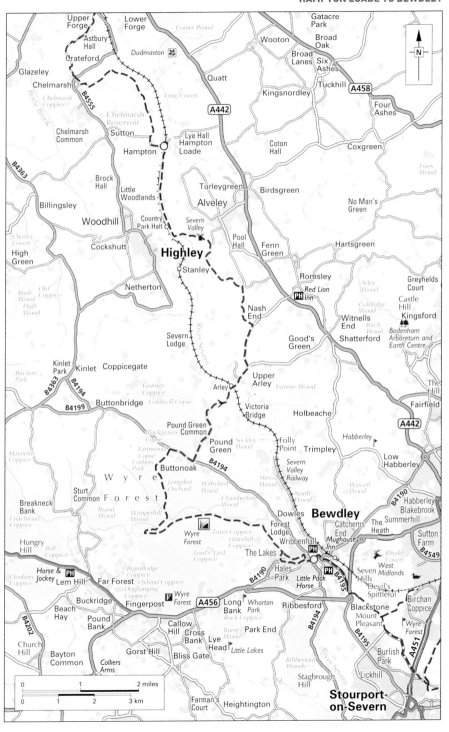

TELFORD TO IRONBRIDGE GORGE

Telford is a new town with an industrial history. It's named after the engineer Thomas Telford, one of the principal architects of the Industrial Revolution, whose mark on this area is clearly visible today.

The route is one of great contrasts, with futuristic new developments, pockets of woodland and meadow, and mature parkland. Part of it is on the Silkin Way, named after Lewis Silkin, an MP who was instrumental in getting the 1949 Access to the Countryside Act passed. It is an excellent cycle route due to the use of canal beds and extinct railway lines, and for the most part the way is well surfaced.

Ironbridge Gorge houses ten indoor and outdoor museums exploring various aspects of the area's social and industrial history. You can buy one 'passport' ticket with no time limit, which will give you entry to all ten museums if you don't get to visit them all in one day. The area is also a significant wildlife habitat, with ancient woodlands cheek-by-jowl with post-industrial landscapes, and with Britain's largest untamed river, the Severn, flowing through it. Ironbridge Gorge has been recognized as a UNESCO World Heritage Site.

Thomas Telford's famous iron bridge

ROUTE INFORMATION
National Routes: 55, 81
Start: Wellington train station.
Finish: Ironbridge Gorge.
Distance: 14.5 miles (23.5km).
Grade: Moderate.
Surface: Tarmac and a disused railway of fine gravel.
Hills: A fairly steep climb when travelling south from Trench Lock to Telford, while the climb up from Coalport to Telford is gradual.

YOUNG & INEXPERIENCED CYCLISTS
The Silkin Way is mainly traffic-free and more suitable for novice cyclists and families than the rest of the ride, which is quite hilly.

REFRESHMENTS
• Lots of choice in Wellington, Telford and Ironbridge Gorge.

THINGS TO SEE & DO
• Sunnycroft, Wellington: late 19th-century gentleman's villa and mini country estate, with pigsties, stables, kitchen garden and

orchards; 01952 242884;
www.nationaltrust.org.uk
- **The Ercall:** ancient oak woodland, with spectacular views and more than 500 million years of history; 01743 284280; www.shropshirewildlifetrust.org.uk
- **Granville Country Park:** one of the largest and most wildlife-diverse areas in Telford; pit mounds, canal, woodland and relics of industrial activity; 01743 284280; www.shropshirewildlifetrust.org.uk
- **Telford Town Park:** covers 450 acres; nature trails, Sites of Special Scientific Interest (SSSIs), sports pitches, lakeside

amphitheatre and several beautiful gardens; 01952 382340; www.telford.gov.uk
- **Iron Bridge:** the world's first bridge made of iron, erected in 1779; www.english-heritage.org.uk
- **Ironbridge Gorge:** regarded as the 'birthplace of industry'; ten museums chart the progress of the Industrial Revolution, and visitors can see and experience what life was like during the late 18th and early 19th centuries; 01952 884391; www.ironbridge.org.uk
- **Buildwas Abbey, close to Ironbridge:** impressive ruins of a Cistercian abbey, with

TELFORD TO IRONBRIDGE GORGE

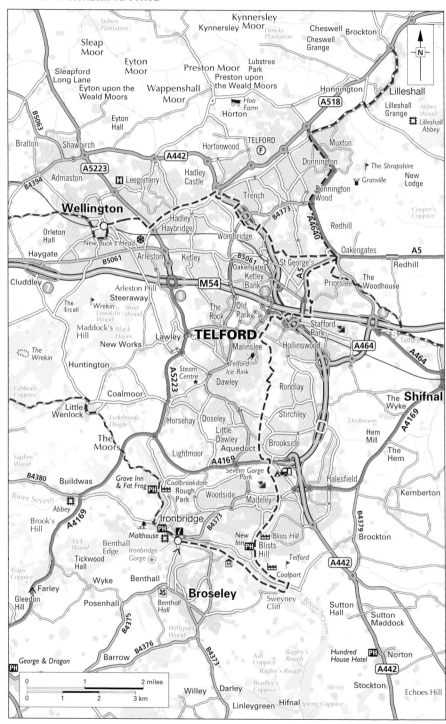

The Museum of Iron

a beautiful vaulted and tile-floored chapter house; the crypt chapel has recently reopened; 01952 433274; www.english-heritage.org.uk

TRAIN STATIONS
Wellington; Oakengates; Telford Central.

BIKE HIRE
- **The Bicycle Hub, Ironbridge:** 01952 883249; www.thebicyclehub.co.uk

FURTHER INFORMATION
- To view or print National Cycle Network routes, visit www.sustrans.org.uk
- Maps for this area are available to buy from www.sustransshop.co.uk
- Telford and Ironbridge Tourist Information: 01952 433424; www.visitironbridge.co.uk
- Shropshire Tourist Information: 01743 281200; www.shropshiretourism.co.uk

ROUTE DESCRIPTION
Come out of Wellington station, turn right onto the Parade and then left onto Victoria Road to join National Route 81. Turn right at the roundabout and then take the first left. Constitution Hill becomes Sutherland Road, then becomes a traffic-free path for a while, going under Whitchurch Drive (A5223), following the Perry Way and joining the Silkin Way at Trench Lock roundabout. It goes back and forth across the Queensway (A442), but stays off-road until it gets to Station Hill. Route 81 then goes left on-road, while the Silkin Way heads traffic-free towards Telford. They both meet up with Route 55.

The Silkin Way takes you under the M54 and on to Rampart Way. Here, it is joined by Route 55 and signposted accordingly. It continues traffic-free through Telford Town Park to Ironbridge Gorge.

NEARBY CYCLE ROUTES
There are a number of cycle trails around Wellington, including the All Round the Wrekin circular trail, which, using existing sections of National Routes 45 and 81, links the small town of Wellington to the Wrekin, a 400m (1,312ft) hill that dominates the landscape. Similarly, the Tern Valley Trail uses Routes 45 and 81 and explores the gently rolling countryside in the tranquil river valleys of the Tern and Roden.

North of the town centre, the Silkin Way intersects with Route 81 and continues to Bratton, while Route 55 goes past Granville Country Park to Newport.

Route 81 goes from Telford via Wellington and Shrewsbury, running across the heart of Mid Wales to Aberystwyth. From Shrewsbury to Aberystwyth, the route is known as Lôn Cambria.

The Mercian Way (Route 45) goes from Ironbridge to Chester, via Whitchurch. You can combine the quiet lanes of the Mercian Way with the disused railway paths of the Silkin Way (Route 55) and the Perry Way (Route 81) for a 36-mile (58km) circuit.

GOBOWEN TO COLEMERE COUNTRY PARK

Experience north Shropshire's wonderful wetlands and canals, and the wealth of wildlife and beautiful countryside surrounding them, on this gentle route. The Meres are wetlands formed by glaciation and are unique in that they have no water flowing in or out of them. They are the remains of Lake Lapworth, an extensive glacial lake that changed the course of the Rivers Dee and Severn. The Mosses, meanwhile, are lowland raised bogs that have, in the recent past, been dug for peat.

This ride takes you from Gobowen, on the edge of Oswestry, through Ellesmere before depositing you in Colemere Country Park, where you can have a picnic or go for a circular walk through woodland glades right along the water's edge.

Ellesmere is a pretty market town with medieval streets, Georgian houses and half-timbered buildings. It is set on the most spectacular of nine glacial meres, and was the birthplace of the Llangollen Canal. This was designed and built by Thomas Telford from his offices in the town. Surrounded by circular walks, woodlands and gardens, the town really is a nature-lover's paradise. It also has antique and gift shops, cafes and traditional inns, plus regular antique markets, festivals and events. If you want to get out on the water, it is possible to hire a boat to drift along the Llangollen Canal.

ROUTE INFORMATION

Regional Route: 31
Start: Gobowen train station.
Finish: Colemere Country Park.
Distance: 14 miles (22.5km).
Grade: Easy.

Surface: Tarmac roads and quiet country lanes.
Hills: Gentle gradients.

YOUNG & INEXPERIENCED CYCLISTS

Suitable for all, though take care on short sections of the B5009, A528 and A495.

Colemere Country Park

REFRESHMENTS
- Tiffins cafe, Derwen College, Gobowen.
- Lots of choice in Ellesmere and Welshampton.
- Picnic area in Colemere Country Park.

THINGS TO SEE & DO
- **Whittington Castle, Gobowen:** the beautiful remains of a 12th-century moated castle, complete with bridge, gatehouse, towers and water frontage; 01691 662500; www.whittingtoncastle.co.uk
- **The Mere, Ellesmere:** picnic area and playground plus cafe and rowing boats for hire in summer; www.visitellesmere.co.uk
- **Colemere:** one of Shropshire's most beautiful meres and a Site of Special Scientific Interest (SSSI); virtually surrounded by mature woodland and two very attractive hay meadows; www.visitellesmere.co.uk
- **Wood Lane, near Colemere:** one of the best bird-watching sites in Shropshire; several large lagoons with islands and surrounding rough grassland; home to lapwings, plovers, tree sparrows and the occasional osprey; 01743 284280; www.shropshirewildlifetrust.org.uk
- **Wem Moss:** access by foot from Northwood, east of Colemere; outstanding example of a lowland raised bog, with monster plants, spiders and snakes; 01743 284280; www.shropshirewildlifetrust.org.uk

TRAIN STATIONS
Gobowen.

BIKE HIRE
None locally.

FURTHER INFORMATION
- To view or print National Cycle Network routes, visit www.sustrans.org.uk
- Maps for this area are available to buy from www.sustransshop.co.uk
- **Ellesmere Tourist Information:** 01691 622981; www.visitellesmere.co.uk
- **North Shropshire Tourist Information:** www.northshropshire.co.uk

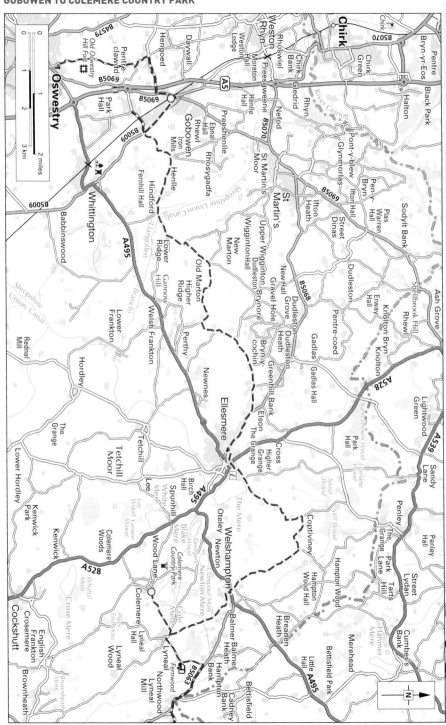

Canal boats on the
Shropshire Union Canal

ROUTE DESCRIPTION

Leave Gobowen train station, turn right onto
Chirk Road, the B5069, and take the next right
onto Old Whittington Road. Regional Route 31
is signed from here to Lyneal.

Be careful as you go along the B5009 and
turn left up Fernhill Lane. This road takes you
through the villages of Hindford and Old Marton
to Ellesmere.

You come into Ellesmere on Elson Road.
Turn left at Brownlow Road. Follow the road
round and briefly go on the A528. Turn left at
Swan Lane. This becomes Swan Hill, and
provides you with beautiful views of the Mere.
Stay on the signposted route going in a
northeasterly direction. The route turns back
south towards Welshampton. You come in on

Stocks Lane, take a left, then a right along the
A495 onto Lyneal Lane and out of the village.
Go over Llangollen Canal and into Lyneal. From
Lyneal, you leave Regional Route 31 and bear
right on entering the village of Colemere, then
take the first left. Following this road brings you
to the lake at Colemere Country Park.

NEARBY CYCLE ROUTES

Regional Route 31 carries on to Whitchurch
from Ellesmere. It converges with the Mercian
Way (National Route 45) southwest of
Whitchurch at Welsh End. In Whitchurch, both
routes follow the Hatton Way disused railway
path to connect with Whitchurch train station.

Route 45 goes north up to Chester or south
down to Salisbury.

STRATFORD GREENWAY

Stratford-upon-Avon is an extremely attractive town dating back to medieval times. As Shakespeare's birthplace, it has retained a rather higher proportion of its historic buildings than most market towns. There is plenty to do, whether you want to watch a play at the Royal Shakespeare Theatre, visit one of the many historic buildings associated with the playwright or just simply sit quietly by the canal.

The Stratford Greenway follows the course of part of the Honeybourne Line, a single-track railway built in 1859 by the Oxford, Worcester & Wolverhampton Railway – its nickname was the Old Worse and Worse. It begins at Seven Meadows Road, where you may be lucky to hear the song of the skylarks, which nest here. The route to the village of Long Marston has become a refuge for wild plants and animals, and as well as fruit and walnut trees, you may spot cowslips, knapweed, wild carrot and tansy.

If you are looking to keep the ride fairly short and traffic-free, Long Marston is the turnaround point. Otherwise, you take the Ilmington circular route, which is mostly flat with some hilly sections. This will take you back to the Stratford Greenway.

ROUTE INFORMATION
National Route: 5
Start and Finish: Stratford-upon-Avon train station.
Distance: 23 miles (37km).
Grade: Medium.
Surface: The Greenway is on a disused railway path, the rest is on quiet roads.
Hills: The Greenway is flat, but the rest is hilly, rolling terrain.

YOUNG & INEXPERIENCED CYCLISTS
The 8 miles (13km) of the Greenway is good for novice cyclists but the rest is suitable only for the more assured cyclist.

REFRESHMENTS
- Lots of choice in Stratford-upon-Avon.
- Cafe set in restored original 1967 GWR railway carriages in Milcote Picnic Area.
- The Masons Arms pub, Long Marston.
- Lots of choice in Ilmington.

THINGS TO SEE & DO
- Anne Hathaway's Cottage, Stratford: actually a substantial, 12-roomed, Elizabethan farmhouse, with its own old-fashioned cottage garden, set in beautiful countryside;

01789 292100; www.shakespeare.org.uk
- Shakespeare's House, Stratford: where the Bard was supposedly born, now restored to its former glory and open to the public; 01789 204016; www.shakespeare.org.uk
- Holy Trinity Church, Stratford: probably England's most-visited parish church as Shakespeare was baptized here, served as a lay rector and is buried in the chancel; 01789 266316; www.stratford-upon-avon.org
- Stratford-upon-Avon Butterfly Farm and

STRATFORD-UPON-AVON

Anne Hathaway's cottage, Stratford

Hidcote Manor Garden

Jungle Safari: Europe's largest butterfly farm; 01789 299288; www.butterflyfarm.co.uk
- **Flowers Wood, near Ilmington**: small rectangular woodland on former pasture, with hawthorn hedges and a circular path; 01476 581135; www.woodlandtrust.org.uk
- **Hidcote Manor Garden, Hidcote Bartrim**: celebrated Arts & Crafts garden; series of outdoor rooms, each with its own unique character; 01386 438333; www.nationaltrust.org.uk
- **Kiftsgate Court Gardens, Mickleton**: series of three interconnecting gardens, with plants from all over the world; harmonious colour schemes and a Mediterranean atmosphere; 01386 438777; www.kiftsgate.co.uk

TRAIN STATIONS
Stratford-upon-Avon.

BIKE HIRE
- **Stratford Bike Hire**: 07711 776340; www.stratfordbikehire.com

FURTHER INFORMATION
- To view or print National Cycle Network routes, visit www.sustrans.org.uk
- Maps for this area are available to buy from www.sustransshop.co.uk
- **Stratford-upon-Avon Tourist Information**: 0870 160 7930; www.shakespeare-country.co.uk

STRATFORD GREENWAY

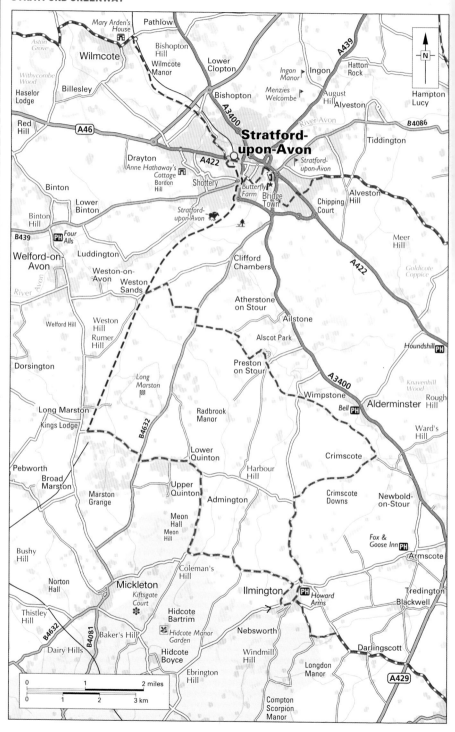

Shakespeare's birthplace

ROUTE DESCRIPTION

Turn right out of Stratford-upon-Avon station and cycle down Station Road. Take a sharp right into Alcester Road and go over the railway bridge. Turn left to join National Route 5 at Stratford College through the car park. You ride along a shared-use path beside Seven Meadows Road to the disused railway line. Heading out into countryside on the traffic-free Stratford Greenway, you cross the River Avon using the multi-span Stannals Bridge.

The kissing gates on Stratford Greenway have been adapted to allow cyclists to push their front wheel into a vertical gap between the hoops, which allows the gate to close behind you. When you get to Long Marston, the route stops being traffic-free at an industrial estate, so turn left onto Station Road and follow the on-road signs to Lower Quinton. Continue straight through the village. Take the first right and climb steadily to the next junction. Go left towards Ilmington. After 2 miles (3km), at the edge of the village, turn right and then left at the next junction.

You leave Ilmington and Route 5, passing the Howard Arms and following the signs to Stratford. After 1.5 miles (2.5km), you turn right towards Crimscote, then left towards Wimpstone. Here, you bear left, then go straight

Crossing the Avon at Stannals Bridge

ahead at the crossroads and straight over at the next one into Preston on Stour. Bear left at the war memorial, then left out of Preston on Stour, follow the road around a few bends and reach a T-junction where you turn left. At the B4632, turn right and shortly afterwards left. Follow this road until you reach a T-junction where you turn left to reach the Stratford Greenway. Turn right to return to Stratford.

NEARBY CYCLE ROUTES

National Route 5 continues southeast through Shipston-on-Stour to Banbury, adding 25 miles (40km) to the ride above. To the north, Route 5 goes from Stratford-upon-Avon to Walsall, via Redditch, Bromsgrove and Birmingham.

Route 41 goes from Long Marston to Rugby, via Stratford-upon-Avon. At Long Marston, the Welford-on-Avon circular returns to Stratford.

REDDITCH TO STRATFORD- UPON-AVON

Redditch grew up from a small hamlet known as 'La Rededich' that had developed around Bordesley Abbey, built by Cistercian monks in the 12th century. The first documented reference to the settlement dates back to 1348. In the 19th century, the town became famous for leading the field in the manufacture of steel needles, while in the early 1960s Redditch was designated a New Town. This led to much redevelopment, including the landscaping of Arrow Valley Country Park. The park extends over 2.5 miles (4km) from Bordesley Abbey in the north to Washford Mill in the south. The River Arrow meanders through the park, providing excellent wildlife habitats and interesting walks for visitors.

This route goes through some of the best countryside that Warwickshire has to offer, on quiet roads, with hardly any hills. There are many interesting attractions, such as Mary Arden's House in Wilmcote and the National Trust properties at Coughton Court, with its close connections to the Gunpowder Plot of 1605, and Kinwarton Dovecote near Alcester.

Mary Arden's House, Wilmcote

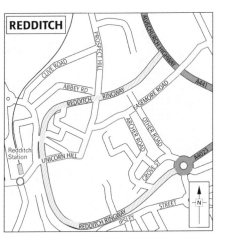

ROUTE INFORMATION

National Route: 5
Start: Redditch train station.
Finish: Stratford-upon-Avon train station.
Distance: 18 miles (29km).
Grade: Easy.
Surface: A mix of greenways and quiet country roads.
Hills: Mostly flat.

YOUNG & INEXPERIENCED CYCLISTS

Suitable for older, cycle-savvy children and adults. Take care on the B4089 into Great Alne.

REFRESHMENTS

- Lots of choice in Redditch.
- The Lark pub, Studley.
- The Holly Bush pub, Alcester.
- Lots of choice in Stratford-upon-Avon.

THINGS TO SEE & DO

- Coughton Court, near Alcester: one of England's finest Tudor country houses, with an impressive gatehouse, beautiful gardens and great vistas of the Warwickshire countryside; 01789 762435; www.coughtoncourt.co.uk
- Kinwarton Dovecote, near Alcester: circular 14th-century building, still with nesting

Coughton Court

doves; 01789 400777;
www.nationaltrust.org.uk
- **Alcester:** ancient Roman town, with preserved Tudor cottages on the High Street, and other historical buildings dotted throughout; www.alcester.co.uk
- **Mary Arden's Farm, Wilmcote:** timbered Tudor farmhouse that was Shakespeare's mother's house, now a Shakespeare countryside museum; www.shakespeare.org.uk

Redditch:
- **Forge Mill Needle Museum:** exhibitions relating to the history of the needle and fishing tackle industries; listed building with original water-powered machinery; 01527 62509; www.forgemill.org.uk
- **Bordesley Abbey:** on the same site as Forge Mill Museum; ruins of a medieval Cistercian Abbey that have been extensively excavated; the visitor centre, set in a 16th-century barn, tells the extraordinary story of the Abbey's development in the 12th century to its destruction in 1538; 01527 62509; www.forgemill.org.uk
- **Arrow Valley Country Park:** 900 acres of green space where you can fish, bird-watch, cycle or indulge in water sports or lakeside

walks; children's play area and a visitor centre; 01527 591106; www.redditch.whub.org.uk
- **The Palace Theatre:** prime example of Edwardian architecture and still in use; 01527 65203; www.redditchpalacetheatre.co.uk

TRAIN STATIONS
Redditch; Stratford-upon-Avon.

BIKE HIRE
- **Stratford Bike Hire:** 07711 776340; www.stratfordbikehire.com

FURTHER INFORMATION
- To view or print National Cycle Network routes, visit www.sustrans.org.uk
- Maps for this area are available to buy from www.sustransshop.co.uk
- **Redditch Tourist Information:** 01527 60806; www.visitworcestershire.org
- **Stratford-upon-Avon Tourist Information:** 0870 160 7930; www.shakespeare-country.co.uk

ROUTE DESCRIPTION
Leave Redditch station through the car park and turn left up the hill on the red-painted cycle

lane. Follow the road right and then left over a toucan crossing and look for the red cycle lane taking you right and down the hill on quiet, traffic-calmed back streets for just under a mile (1.6km). Turn right into the park. This off-road route quickly branches left over a small bridge, and is well signed and picturesque as you travel through parkland alongside the River Arrow.

You will soon come to Arrow Valley Lake, a popular and busy picnic spot with a cafe and play area. Arrow Valley Country Park gives way to paths alongside roads that take you to the edge of Redditch, where the countryside starts. Turn left onto the Greenway alongside Nine Days Lane. The route follows the Greenway for just over half a mile (0.8km) and then joins a quiet lane. The ride is made up of quiet rural roads from here on, passing through the villages of Studley, Coughton and Great Alne.

Be particularly careful on the B road into Great Alne; the traffic is quite fast.

After Wilmcote, which has the only significant hill on this ride, turn onto the Stratford-upon-Avon Canal. Follow the canal for a couple of miles (3km). The exit is a few hundred metres (yards) after a road crossing. Turn right over Timothy's Bridge Road, then left onto Mason's Road. Follow this to Alcester Road and go left. Route 5 goes right, but you go straight over the roundabout for Stratford-upon-Avon station.

NEARBY CYCLE ROUTES

National Route 5 carries on through Stratford, passing Holy Trinity Church (where Shakespeare is buried) and then on the Greenway route for a further 5 miles (8km) to Long Marston (see page 34). It continues on-road to Banbury and beyond. To the north, it goes to Bromsgrove, Birmingham and Walsall.

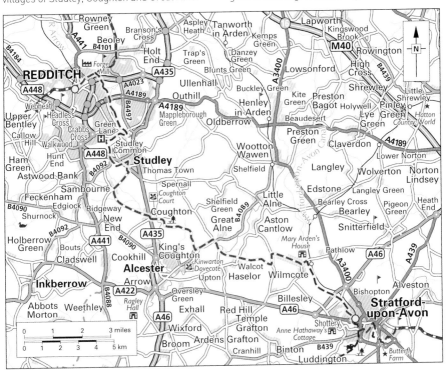

PLANTSBROOK VALLEY

The Plantsbrook Valley is a wonderful area of green open space running through northeast Birmingham between Sutton Coldfield and Castle Vale. It is large enough to be considered as the local countryside for communities in the area, providing peaceful relaxation and the chance for recreational activities. In 2011 a new cycling and walking route was built, linking local communities to the valley and providing access to schools, hospitals, New Hall Valley Country Park, Sutton Coldfield town centre, the enormous Sutton Park and, at its southern end, the Birmingham & Fazeley Canal towpath. At the northern end of the route there are links to new walking and cycling routes across Rectory Park to Good Hope Hospital. From the top of the New Hall Valley Country Park a new route will branch off to give a safe and secure link all the way through Sutton Coldfield town centre to Sutton Park, one of the largest urban parks in Europe (it is even bigger than Richmond Park in London). The park's 2,400 acres include a mix of heathland, wetlands and marshes, seven lakes, extensive ancient woodlands, several restaurants, a municipal golf course, a donkey sanctuary, children's playgrounds and a visitor centre. To the south, the route goes through Pype Hayes, one of Birmingham's biggest parks, to Plantsbrook Local Nature Reserve, a wildlife haven consisting of open water, wetland, woodland and meadow.

*Sutton Park
in autumn*

PLANTSBROOK VALLEY
SUTTON COLDFIELD TO PYPE HAYES PARK

ROUTE INFORMATION
National Route: 534
Start and Finish: Sutton Coldfield station;
Rectory Park; Plantsbrook Local Nature
Reserve.
Distance: 6 miles (9.5km).
Grade: Easy.
Surface: Well-surfaced cyclepaths.
Hills: None.

YOUNG & INEXPERIENCED CYCLISTS
The route from Rectory Park to Plantsbrook
Local Nature Reserve is traffic-free and ideal
for children and novices. Routes within Sutton
Park are also traffic-free. A link from the route
direct to Sutton Park is being developed.
Currently it is accessed by local roads which
may not be suitable for cyclists of all abilities.

*A safe route through
Sutton Coldfield*

REFRESHMENTS
- Plenty of options in Sutton Coldfield.
Within Sutton Park you will find:
- Blackroot Bistro: 0121 355 2570;
  www.blackrootbistro.co.uk
- The Boathouse at Bracebridge Restaurant:
  0121 308 8890
- Town Gate Café: 0121 354 6791

THINGS TO SEE & DO
- Pilkington Donkey Centre, Sutton Park:
  0121 354 9444; www.elisabethsvendsentrust.
  org.uk
- Walking and cycling routes throughout
  Sutton Park.
- Sutton Park Model Aero Club:
  www.spmac.net
- Pype Hayes Park: numerous facilities
  including tennis courts, play area,
  ornamental gardens and fishing ponds.
- Plantsbrook Local Nature Reserve: open
  water, wetland, woodland and meadow;
  0121 351 7007

TRAIN STATIONS
Chester Road; Sutton Coldfield; Wylde Green.

BIKE HIRE
- JJ's Cycle Shop, Sutton Coldfield:
  0121 354 8810; www.cycles4all.co.uk

Old Turn Junction, Birmingham

FURTHER INFORMATION

- To view or print National Cycle Network routes, visit www.sustrans.org.uk
- Maps for this area are available to buy from www.sustransshop.co.uk
- Birmingham Tourist Information: www.visitbirmingham.com

ROUTE DESCRIPTION

The best place to start this linear ride is from Sutton Coldfield station, where there are trains from Birmingham every 10 minutes during the day. Leave the station from the main entrance and head right, along Railway Road. At the T-junction with High Street turn right, then first left into Midland Drive. Follow this one-way street until you reach the T-junction with Rectory Road, where you turn left and follow the road until you see the entrance to Rectory Park on your right, immediately opposite Good Hope Hospital. In the park, follow signs for the National Cycle Network Route 534 south, crossing Reddicap Hill and continuing into the unspoilt New Hall Valley Country Park, where it is hard to believe you are in Britain's second largest city. The route continues south across Wylde Green Road and Penns Lane and alongside Plants Brook. Here, superb paths lead to Pype Hayes Park, which is a fabulous place to visit in autumn to see both the seasonal colours of the trees and shrubs and Birmingham's largest bonfire and fireworks display. The route then crosses Tyburn Road opposite Plantsbrook Local Nature Reserve before joining the towpath of the Birmingham &Fazeley Canal.

If you are heading to Sutton Park from Sutton Coldfield station, leave the station on the north side via the main car park, turning left onto Railway Road. Turn right at the T-junction with Park Road and continue straight on into Tudor Hill, where the main park entrance is on your left.

NEARBY CYCLE ROUTES

The entire new route is signed as National Cycle Network Route 534 and will link into National Route 535, which runs into Birmingham City centre.

There are several local routes throughout Sutton Park and Castle Vale as well as the nearby Ward End route. Cycling is also permitted on the Birmingham and Fazeley Canal towpath.

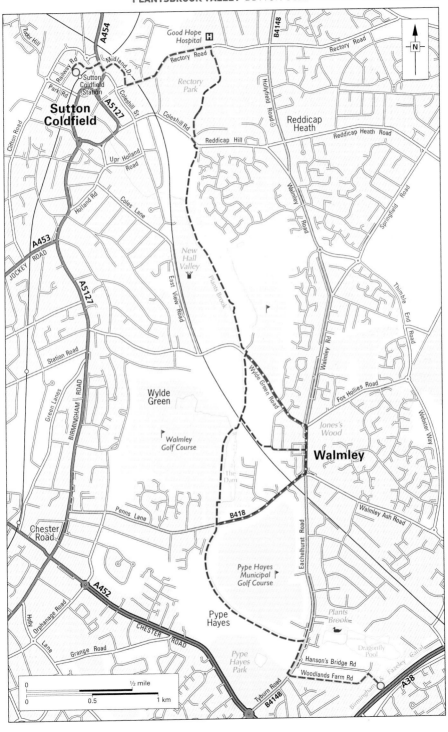

THE LIAS LINE CYCLEWAY

This attractive route from the centre of Rugby follows the Great Central Way to the outskirts of town. Built upon a dismantled railway track, it takes you to the Wildlife Trust site at Ashlawn Cutting, which is a haven for rare plants and butterflies. It also passes the Warwickshire Wildlife Trust sites at Cock Robin Wood and Windmill Spinney.

On reaching the reservoir and country park of Draycote Water, a 5-mile (8km) path runs all the way around this delightful watery attraction, which is the ideal place for a lunch stop. Once back in the saddle, the attractive village of Offchurch is a worthwhile distraction on the outskirts of Leamington Spa. Here, the park of Newbold Comyn offers a beguiling combination of open land, woodland and wetlands beside the River Leam, before joining the Grand Union Canal and passing the Leam Valley wildlife site.

The elegant town of Leamington Spa boomed at the turn of the 19th century, when the commercial potential of its saline springs was discovered. In both Leamington Spa and Warwick, the route passes the station, meaning the return journey could be made by train. Lock up bikes at Warwick station and take a stroll through Priory Park to its historic centre, where you are only moments from one of the finest medieval castles in England.

ROUTE INFORMATION
National Route: 41
Start: Rugby train station.
Finish: Warwick train station.
Distance: 23 miles (37km).
Grade: Easy.
Surface: Tarmac or fine gravel paths.

Hills: Fairly flat.

YOUNG & INEXPERIENCED CYCLISTS
Mostly traffic-free, with some on-road sections. Take care crossing the B4455 and A425.

REFRESHMENTS
- Lots of choice in Rugby.
- Cafe and picnic area at Draycote Water.
- Pubs on the canal section of the ride near Long Itchington.

Jogging along the Lias Line

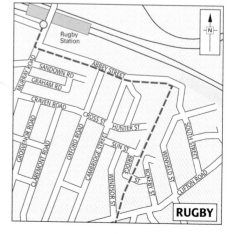

Warwick Castle

- Newbold Comyn Arms pub, Newbold Comyn.
- Lots of choice in Leamington Spa and Warwick.

THINGS TO SEE & DO

- **Ashlawn Cutting, Rugby:** nature reserve, with 24 species of butterfly, wildflowers and ponds that support frogs, toads, newts and dragonflies; 024 7630 2912; www.warwickshire-wildlife-trust.org.uk
- **Cock Robin Wood, Bilton:** nature reserve, which includes a pond and a sculpture trail; 024 7630 2912; www.warwickshire-wildlife-trust.org.uk
- **Draycote Water:** picturesque reservoir with a country park, facilities for anglers, bird-watchers, walkers and sailboarders; visitor centre; 01788 811153; www.draycotewater.co.uk
- **Draycote Meadows:** Site of Special Scientific Interest (SSSI); two beautiful species-rich hay meadows, with swathes of wildflowers in spring and summer; 01926 811193 www.warwickshire-wildlife-trust.org.uk
- **Newbold Comyn:** extensive park for informal recreation, sport and wildlife; 01926 450000; www.warwickdc.gov.uk
- **Leam Valley:** nature reserve that includes

LEAMINGTON SPA

WARWICK

Leamington Spa's
red-brick Town Hall

woodland, grassland, marsh and ponds;
particularly valuable for birds, butterflies
and dragonflies; 024 7630 2912
www.warwickshire-wildlife-trust.org.uk
• Royal Pump Rooms, Leamington Spa:
award-winning art gallery and museum,
including local history; 01926 742700;
www.warwickdc.gov.uk
• Lord Leycester Hospital, Warwick: historic
group of 14th-century timber-framed
buildings clustered round the Norman
gateway into Warwick; 01926 491422;
www.lordleycester.com
• Warwick Castle: built during the reign of
William the Conqueror; due to extensive
rebuilding and restoration work, it is now a
working castle and a living museum of the
life and times of several periods of history;
0871 265 2000; www.warwick-castle.com

TRAIN STATIONS
Rugby; Leamington Spa; Warwick.

BIKE HIRE
None locally.

FURTHER INFORMATION
• To view or print National Cycle Network
routes, visit www.sustrans.org.uk
• Maps for this area are available to buy from
www.sustransshop.co.uk
• Rugby Tourist Information: 01788 534970;
www.rugby.gov.uk
• Warwick Tourist Information: 01926 492212;
www.warwickdc.gov.uk

ROUTE DESCRIPTION
From Rugby station, turn left, then right onto
Murray Road, and then left again onto Abbey
Street. There is a signed access point onto the
Lias Line Cycleway just before the road bends
to the right. Take the zigzag path up beside
Ashlawn Road Bridge to continue alongside
Ashlawn Road. Be careful not to miss this, as
it's quite easy to continue down Great Central
Way. After a mix of on-road sections and
bridleways, you arrive at Draycote Water.
The route is signed both ways round the
reservoir. Left is towards the visitor centre;

A welcome break on
the Lias Line

Taking a break at Draycote Water

right continues directly towards Leamington.

A traffic-free track leads from the reservoir to the road at Draycote village. Turn right here, past Draycote Meadows, and continue to a railway bridge. Join the railway path and enjoy a traffic-free ride as far as Birdingbury station (now a private house). You pass along quiet country lanes through the beautiful village of Birdingbury, and continue to join the path along the Grand Union Canal, past Long Itchington. A further section of disused railway path is joined before the route follows lanes to Offchurch. This part of the route crosses the Fosse Way (B4455) – take care at this junction.

The ride continues along a railway path, which takes you back to the canal towpath. You then enter Leamington Spa (take care crossing the A425) through Newbold Comyn park. The route continues through Leamington on-road.

Take care on this busy section past the Pump Rooms, into Spencer Street and round to Leamington Spa station. Carry on to Warwick station where the delightful route from Leamington is part on-road, part off-road, and includes the path through St Nicholas Park.

NEARBY CYCLE ROUTES
National Route 41 goes south down to Stratford-upon-Avon, where it meets Route 5. There you can ride the Stratford Greenway (see page 34) or go on the West Midlands Cycle Route that runs from Oxford to Nottingham.

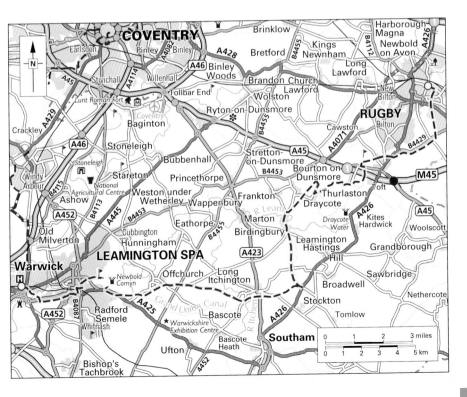

AROUND MARKET BOSWORTH

Market Bosworth itself is a picturesque and historic market town, while the surrounding area is very unspoilt and scenic, with many interesting villages, attractions and leisure facilities. It is also the site of the Battle of Bosworth in 1485, a major turning point in history, where Richard III lost his crown and life to Henry Tudor in one of the last great encounters of the Wars of the Roses. As well as sign-boarded walks around the battlefield, the Bosworth Battlefield Heritage Centre provides a complete insight into the battle and the medieval age in which it took place.

This peaceable corner of the Leicestershire countryside is a district famous among knowing riders but otherwise it's a hidden gem. The route crosses over the 22-mile (35km) long Ashby Canal, as it meanders gently through the very level countryside. Hedgerows and reeds give an air of timelessness, while offering ideal habitats for many species of wildlife. The route passes some fascinating villages along the way, including Stoke Golding, which has a fine 13th-century church and is known as the 'birthplace of the Tudor dynasty'. It was here that Henry Tudor was crowned king following the Battle of Bosworth.

ROUTE INFORMATION

National Route: 52
Start and Finish: Market Bosworth Square.
Distance: 12 miles (19.5km).
Grade: Easy.
Surface: Quiet country lanes.
Hills: None.

YOUNG & INEXPERIENCED CYCLISTS

Ideal for novice cyclists and families.

REFRESHMENTS

- Lots of choice in Market Bosworth.
- Lakeside cafe at Bosworth Water Trust (summer only).
- Cafe at Shenton station.
- Pubs and a general store in Stoke Golding.
- Cafe at Whitemoors Antique Centre, Shenton.

THINGS TO SEE & DO

- **Market Bosworth Country Park:** a landscaped 86-acre park with a lake, planted arboretum with exotic species, wildflower meadow and community woodland; 0116 305 5000; www.leics.gov.uk
- **Bosworth Battlefield Heritage Centre & Country Park:** includes the Battlefield Trail; special events throughout summer; film theatre, gift shop, picnic areas and cafe; 01455 290429; www.bosworthbattlefield.com
- **Bosworth Water Trust:** 50-acre leisure park between Wellsborough and Market Bosworth

Bosworth Battlefield

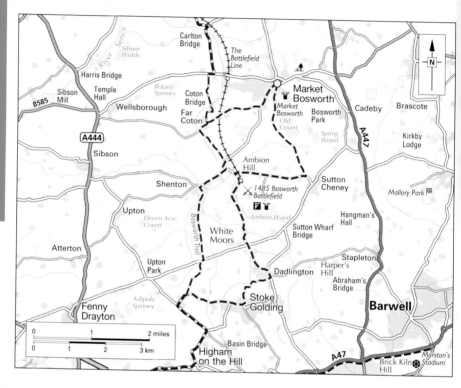

with 20 acres for water sports, including sailing, windsurfing, kayaking and fishing; small entrance charge; 01455 291876; www.bosworthwatertrust.co.uk
- Shenton station: located in the centre of Bosworth Field; steam trains run a 10-mile (16km) round trip in summer to Shackerstone, which has a museum and cafe; walks link it to the Battlefield Heritage Centre; 01827 880754; www.battlefield-line-railway.co.uk
- Ashby Canal: the towpath links Market Bosworth and Hinckley and is an important wildlife corridor for kingfishers, herons and water voles; boat trips available; 0845 671 5530; www.waterscape.com

TRAIN STATIONS
Hinckley; Nuneaton; Leicester.

BIKE HIRE
None locally.

FURTHER INFORMATION
- To view or print National Cycle Network routes, visit www.sustrans.org.uk
- Maps for this area are available to buy from www.sustransshop.co.uk
- Bosworth Cycle Rides: 01455 212416; www.whitesg.plus.com/bosworthcycle/
- Leicestershire Tourist Information: 0116 225 4000; www.goleicestershire.com

ROUTE DESCRIPTION
From Market Bosworth Square, go south, past the Black Horse pub and carry straight on to join Sutton Lane. At the first junction, just outside Sutton Cheney, turn sharp right onto

Narrowboats on the Ashby Canal

Ambion Lane, to pass the Battlefield Centre, half a mile (0.8km) later on the left-hand side. At the T-junction, just beyond the railway bridge, turn left and go past Shenton station.

Follow the road over the next crossroads (Fenn Lanes – take care here) and into Dadlington. After the village green in Dadlington, turn right at the crossroads onto Stoke Lane, go downhill to the canal and then through Stoke Golding to The George pub. At the junction by the pub, turn right and follow Station Road downhill and over the canal and railway bridges. Take the next right, where you join National Route 52, and follow Foxcovert Lane to the next junction. This is a staggered crossroads, where you go right, then left to follow Mill Lane past Whitemoors Centre and into Shenton. Take the next right over the little river bridge and pass Shenton Hall on your right. Go under the aqueduct and turn immediately left.

After a sharp right bend, take the next left and follow the road until you arrive at a T-junction by a canal bridge. Turn right up the hill into Far Coton, where you leave Route 52 and carry straight on to the next T-junction. Turn left and follow Shenton Lane back into Bosworth, turning left to take you back to the market square.

NEARBY CYCLE ROUTES

National Route 52 goes north to Snibston Discovey Park in Coalville. It crosses Route 63, which goes west to Conkers Centre at Moira (in the National Forest) and east to Leicester, Oakham and Rutland Water on a mixture of cycle paths and minor roads.

Route 52 goes south to Nuneaton.

Memorial stone at Bosworth

BRAMPTON VALLEY WAY

This is one of the longest dismantled railway paths in the region, connecting Market Harborough with the outskirts of Northampton near Kingsthorpe and forming part of Route 6 of the National Cycle Network. It is a wide, well-maintained trail with few barriers, making it a perfect 'conversational' ride: a chance to catch up with friends while getting some exercise. The trail includes two tunnels, where you will need lights. There are some old steam locomotives and rolling stock at Chapel Brampton. After the railway line was closed in 1981, it was purchased by Northamptonshire County Council in 1987 and opened for recreational use as the Brampton Valley Way in 1993. Named after the Brampton Arm, a tributary of the River Nene, the railway path follows the river valley for much of its length.

There are two other nearby traffic-free rides: an arm of the Grand Union Canal leads northwest from Market Harborough towards Foxton Locks; also, at the southern end of this route, there is a waymarked link on bridleways and quiet lanes to the circuit of Pitsford Water and Brixworth Country Park.

ROUTE INFORMATION
National Route: 6
Start: Market Harborough train station.
Finish: Boughton Crossing near Kingsthorpe, just north of Northampton.
Distance: 14 miles (22.5km).
Grade: Easy.
Surface: Rolled stone paths.

Hills: Gentle railway gradients; no steep hills.

YOUNG & INEXPERIENCED CYCLISTS
Nearly all the route is off-road but with some crossings, especially at Lamport, where care is needed and children should be closely supervised.

REFRESHMENTS
• Lots of choice in Market Harborough.
• The Bulls Head pub in Arthingworth, just off the route.

Oxendon Tunnel on the Brampton Valley Way

MARKET HARBOROUGH

Cottesbrooke Hall and gardens

- Pitsford & Brampton station.
- The Windhover family pub at Boughton Crossing.

THINGS TO SEE & DO
- **Market Harborough:** attractive market town with a wealth of Georgian architecture.
- **Kelmarsh Hall:** 18th-century historic house, set in beautiful gardens; 01604 686543; www.kelmarsh.com
- **Cottesbrooke Hall:** Queen Anne house (1702), reputed to be Jane Austen's inspiration for *Mansfield Park*; 01604 505808; www.cottesbrookehall.co.uk
- **Lamport Hall, Gardens and Farm Museum:** Grade I listed building, home to the Isham family for more than 400 years; 01604 686272; www.lamporthall.co.uk

- **Brixworth Country Park:** visitor centre, nature trails and scenic picnic sites; www.northamptonshire.gov.uk
- **Northampton & Lamport Steam Railway:** at Pitsford & Brampton Station; 01604 820327; www.nlr.org.uk

TRAIN STATIONS
Market Harborough.

BIKE HIRE
- **Pitsford Cycle Hire, Brixworth Country Park:** 01604 881777; www.pitsfordcycles.co.uk

FURTHER INFORMATION
- To view or print National Cycle Network routes, visit www.sustrans.org.uk
- Maps for this area are available to buy from

Easy riding on the railway path

www.sustransshop.co.uk
- **Northamptonshire Tourist Information:** www.britainonshow.co.uk
- **Market Harborough Tourist Information:** 01858 821270
- **Northampton Tourist Information:** 01604 622 677; www.britainonshow.co.uk

ROUTE DESCRIPTION

From Market Harborough station, head westwards on Rockingham Road (A4304) and left at the traffic lights into Kettering Road, which becomes Springfield Street. Turn left and directly right into Britannia Walk. The path starts at the southern end of Britannia Walk, runs alongside Oaklands Park and crosses Scotland Road, where you need to take care. You soon reach rolling countryside, climbing gently to the Oxendon Tunnel (use your lights) before crossing the flat valley of the River Ise.

For a refreshment break, take the byway to the left just before the Ise Bridge and follow it into Arthingworth, a pretty village with a good pub. Turn right onto Kelmarsh Road at the edge of the village and follow it to the picnic site, where you rejoin the railway path. Alternatively, cross the railway path and continue on Kelmarsh Road to meet Kelmarsh Hall. Continuing southwards on the railway path,

ride through woodlands and beneath High Northamptonshire via Kelmarsh Tunnel (again, use your lights). Take care crossing the A508 south of the tunnel. Just before Brixworth you can take a detour to Cottesbrooke Hall by turning right at the Brixworth–Creaton Road crossing. Alternatively, turn left into Brixworth for Brixworth Country Park. Back on the railway path, you cycle alongside the Northampton & Lamport Steam Railway before reaching the end of the ride at Boughton Crossing, just north of Kingsthorpe on the A5199.

NEARBY CYCLE ROUTES

National Route 6 runs south to Milton Keynes and Oxford. North, it heads for Leicester, Loughborough and Derby. National Route 64 diverges from Route 6 in Market Harborough and follows mostly quiet lanes over High Leicestershire to Melton Mowbray (see page 62), crossing the Leicester–Oakham–Rutland Water section of Route 63.

Other waymarked or traffic-free routes include:
- Great Central Way, Riverside and Watermead Park, Leicester.
- Rutland Water Circuit near Oakham, off National Route 63 (see page 58).

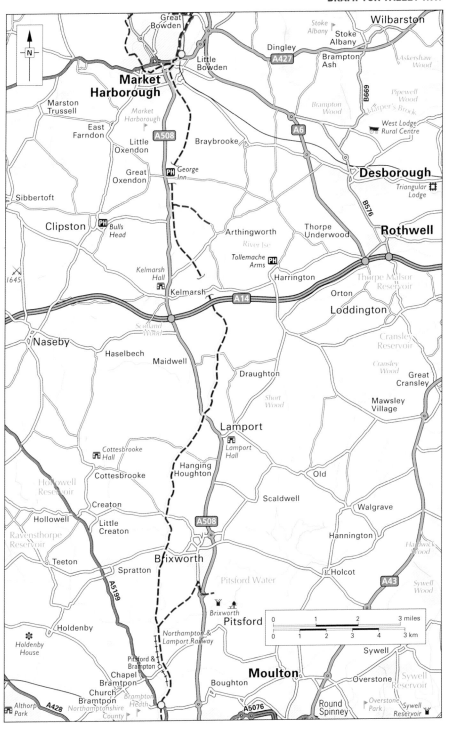

RUTLAND WATER CIRCUIT

Rutland, famously England's smallest county, has at its heart one of England's largest man-made lakes, created as a reservoir in the 1970s. The ride begins in historic Oakham, with its Norman castle site, 16th-century school and County Museum.

Besides beautiful scenery and stunning countryside, high spots include a possible detour to Barnsdale Gardens created by the late Geoff Hamilton, the television gardening presenter. The half-drowned Normanton Church is also a sight not to miss, being the last remnant of a village depopulated in the 18th century to make way for a park. The foundations of the village are under water but the upper parts of the church are still visible, housing an exhibition on the making of the lake.

Rutland Water itself is an attractive 3,100-acre reservoir, with a mature balance of leisure facilities and wildlife conservation. You can try various water sports or rock-climbing, hire a dinghy, bicycle or fishing boat, visit the Egleton and Lyndon nature reserves, or just relax by the water and watch the action around the 25-mile (40km) shoreline.

ROUTE INFORMATION
National Route: 63 and Rutland Water Circuit
Start and Finish: Oakham train station.
Distance: 17 miles (27.5km). Additional alternative via Upper Hambleton Island 7 miles (11km).
Grade: Mostly easy.
Surface: Tarmac roads and stone-surfaced paths.
Hills: No long drags but a few sharp climbs.

YOUNG & INEXPERIENCED CYCLISTS
Mainly traffic-free but with some on-road sections.

REFRESHMENTS
• Lots of choice in Oakham, including The Grainstore Brewery pub.
• Cafe and picnic area at Edith Weston.

THINGS TO SEE & DO
• Oakham Castle: one of the finest examples of late 12th-century domestic architecture in England; 01572 758440; www.rutnet.co.uk
• All Saints Church, Oakham: 14th-century spire; inside, the capitals of the nave arcades depict various grotesque figures, animals, angels and scenes from the Bible; 01572

Normanton Church, Rutland Water

724007; www.allsaintsoakham.org.uk

- **Rutland County Museum, Oakham:** displays of archaeology, history and rural life; cafe in the 200-year-old indoor riding school; award-winning garden; 01572 758440; www.rutland.gov.uk/museum
- **Barnsdale Gardens, Oakham:** 37 individual gardens, including rose, Japanese, rock, knot, kitchen and bog gardens, and an orchard; 01572 813200; www.barnsdalegardens.co.uk
- **Rutland Water Nature Reserve:** one of the most important wildfowl sanctuaries in Great Britain, with more than 20,000 waterfowl; a Site of Special Scientific Interest (SSSI) and internationally recognized as a globally important wetland; 01572 770651; www.rutlandwater.org.uk
- **Normanton Church, Rutland Water:** houses a museum and exhibition on the building of the reservoir; 01572 653026; www.rutnet.co.uk
- **Egleton Nature Reserve:** internationally famous nature reserve, with environmental displays, viewing gallery and 22 bird hides and nature trails; 01572 770651; www.lrwt.org.uk

TRAIN STATIONS
Oakham.

BIKE HIRE
- **Rutland Cycling, Normanton Car Park:**

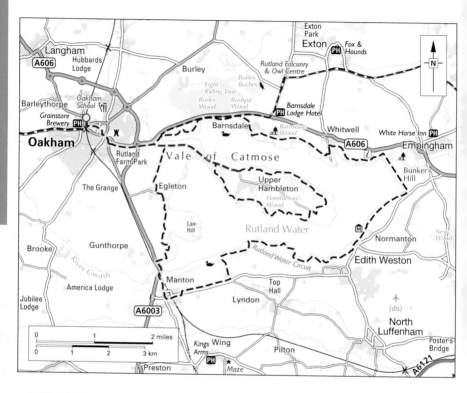

01780 720888; and at Whitwell Leisure Park:
01780 460705; www.rutlandcycling.com

FURTHER INFORMATION

- To view or print National Cycle Network routes, visit www.sustrans.org.uk
- Maps for this area are available to buy from www.sustransshop.co.uk
- Oakham Tourist Information: 01780 686800; www.rutnet.co.uk
- Rutland Water Tourist Information: 01572 770651; www.rutlandwater.org.uk

ROUTE DESCRIPTION

Leaving Oakham station (Stamford platform side), turn right onto the B668, then left onto Northgate Street. At the T-junction with Church Street, go straight over, dismount and push through to Market Place on the footpath, with the church on the left. In Market Place, watch out for the old roofed town pump and the stocks beneath the medieval Butter Market.

Follow Market Place round to the right, turn left onto the bustling High Street, go straight over the traffic lights and into Catmos Street, which veers to the right at the mini-roundabout to become the A6003. Then, just past the left turn into Rutland Council's car park, watch for a path on the left, behind a grey barrier-fence, with a blue bike-and-pedestrian sign. Take this, keeping watchful at the blind bend, then turn right onto the path beside Stamford Road, clearly signed as National Route 63.

Remain on the path, go past a new roundabout and onwards alongside the A606 as far as the turning to Egleton and Hambleton. Go right here, then right again, watching out

Barnsdale Gardens

for the green and cream signs for Egleton Nature Reserve and Normanton. Once here, follow the circuit anticlockwise around the lake.

Now you're spoiled for choice of things to do and see, including spotting ospreys in the bird hides, visiting country inns, visitor centres, boat rides and the broad, ever-changing perspectives of the lake itself. To help decide what's for you, pick up an *Activities at Rutland Water* pamphlet at Oakham Museum or Egleton Bird Watching Centre.

Although most of the route is easy, two tricky spots remain. Under the railway bridge, beside the A6003, the path is narrow. Watch out for people coming the other way. Then, beyond Manton, there is a short section of the busy road to Edith Weston before turning left again, back onto the circuit proper.

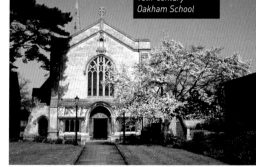

16th-century Oakham School

NEARBY CYCLE ROUTES

To the west, National Route 63 climbs on-lane over the fine landscapes of high Leicestershire to the city of Leicester. On the way, you run for a while on the same alignment as the Melton Mowbray to Market Harborough section of Route 64 (see page 62).

GARTREE RIDE

The name of this ride comes from the old Saxon administrative district of Gartree Hundred. The ride zigzags from one country town to another, through pleasant villages and quintessentially English countryside with long views.

Market Harborough is a rare medieval 'new town' – its market was established in the 12th century to boost local trade. Local gems on display in the Harborough Museum include one of the largest hoards of Iron Age and Roman coins ever found in Britain.

Melton Mowbray is also an historic market town, once one of Britain's trendiest inland resorts and still famous for its cheeses and, of course, pork pies. If you've time, ride up to Melton Country Park, which boasts a valuable wildlife habitat, sports pitches, play areas, picnic places and a visitor centre with a cafe.

ROUTE INFORMATION
National Routes: 64, 63
Start: Market Harborough train station.
Finish: Melton Mowbray train station.
Distance: 24 miles (38.5km).
Grade: Difficult.
Surface: Mostly on-lane.
Hills: Steep rolling countryside.

YOUNG & INEXPERIENCED CYCLISTS
Suitable for children aged 11 and over, with some road-riding experience and a good spread of gears, and accompanied by adults.

REFRESHMENTS
- Lots of choice in Market Harborough and Melton Mowbray.
- The Red Lion pub, Welham.
- Other pubs en route.

THINGS TO SEE & DO
Market Harborough:
- St Dionysius: 14th-century church with a superb spire that is one of the finest in England; 01858 469330; www.harborough-anglican.org.uk
- The Old Grammar School: unusual 17th-century timber-framed building standing on massive oak pillars; 01858 821085; www.leics.gov.uk
- Harborough Museum: includes the Southeast Leicestershire Treasure, one of the most significant Iron Age finds in Britain; 01858 821085; www.leics.gov.uk

Melton Mowbray:
- Melton Carnegie Museum: displays on matters of local interest, including cheese-making, pies and fox-hunting; 0116 305 3860; www.leics.gov.uk
- St Mary's Church: the most magnificent in Leicestershire; 01664 562267; www.melton.leicester.anglican.org
- Melton Country Park: 140 acres of informal parkland and a lake, with picnic sites, cycle tracks, nature trails and children's play areas; www.melton.gov.uk

TRAIN STATIONS
Market Harborough; Melton Mowbray.

BIKE HIRE
None locally.

FURTHER INFORMATION
- To view or print National Cycle Network routes, visit www.sustrans.org.uk
- Maps for this area are available to buy from www.sustransshop.co.uk
- Market Harborough Tourist Information: 01858 828282; www.harborough.gov.uk
- Melton Mowbray Tourist Information: 01664 480992; www.melton.co.uk
- Leicestershire Tourist Information: 01455 635106; www.goleicestershire.com

Market Harborough's Old Grammar School

ROUTE DESCRIPTION

Turn right from Market Harborough station onto Great Bowden Road, following signs for National Route 64, which take you all the way to Melton. Leaving Great Bowden for Welham, you cross the A6 and head into open country. A footbridge takes you over a tributary of the River Welland. After Welham, head for Cranoe. From the crossroads (straight over), just before the village, climb sharply towards a steep left-hander, bending between steep banks and shady trees around the churchyard.

The gradient eases before pitching sharply down again to Glooston, where you turn right. The single track between Glooston and Goadby is steep and winding, with cattle grids; it can be muddy. In Goadby, turn right and take the road towards Tugby. Go right at the following

Melton Mowbray pork pie shop

junction, where you join National Route 63. At the next crossroads, go left for Tugby.

Take very great care when crossing the fast, busy A47, just north of Tugby. Ride the switchback beyond, keeping your eyes peeled when going straight over the next two crossroads. Next comes a staggered left-then-

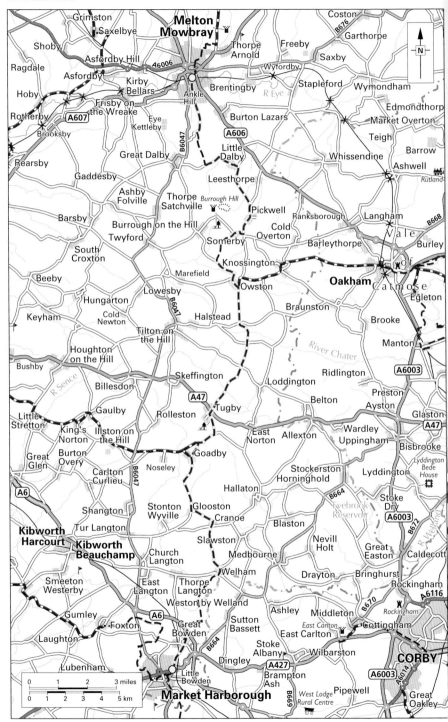

St Mary's Church,
Melton Mowbray

right near Whatborough Farm, where traffic can be unexpectedly busy, so be especially vigilant. At Owston, turn left down Main Street and ride on via Newbold to Somerby. Much of this section is single track, and care is needed to avoid potholes and the like.

Burrough Hill is an Iron Age fort and country park about a mile (1.6km) northwest of Somerby – it's well worth the detour if you've time. Otherwise, at the eastern end of Somerby, turn left for Pickwell, where you veer left for Little Dalby. Go left at the next junction, then left again through Little Dalby itself. Although you're now heading towards Great Dalby, watch carefully for the Route 64 sign inviting you to turn right up the steep track over Gartree Hill. Hard work but great views! When you reach Melton Mowbray, keep on along Route 64 until

the A606 (Burton Road) junction. Here you are advised to turn left, dismount and walk over the railway using the pedestrian footbridge. Immediately after, you double back sharp left for Melton Mowbray station and journey's end.

NEARBY CYCLE ROUTES
National Route 6 goes south from Market Harborough via the Brampton Valley Way (see page 54), mostly traffic-free, to Northampton.

From Goadby, Route 63 heads west for Leicester and, from Owston, east to Oakham and Rutland Water on a mixture of cyclepaths and minor roads.

From Melton Mowbray, Route 64 continues on-lane to Woolsthorpe by Belvoir, where it turns right for the Mucky Duck pub en route to Grantham, via the canal towpath and Route 15.

GREAT CENTRAL WAY

Leicester boasts an ancient tradition of cultural diversity to match any in the land, and its strategic location as a military and administrative centre was recognized by the Romans and later by the Danes.

This ride runs from the southern suburb of Blaby, skirts the city centre and extends via the National Space Centre to reach the bird-rich, willow-fringed lakes of Watermead Park in the north.

Much of the route is traffic-free, though you do need to stay vigilant at several road crossings along the way. Leicester's wider cycling network is one of the best in Britain and its city centre incorporates what is said to be Europe's largest cycle-friendly pedestrian zone.

ROUTE INFORMATION

National Routes: 6, 48
Start: Northfield Park, Blaby.
Finish: Watermead Park, Syston.
Distance: 10 miles (16km).
Grade: Easy.
Surface: Mostly tarmac.
Hills: For the most part fairly flat, with one short climb in Glen Parva.

YOUNG & INEXPERIENCED CYCLISTS

A few sections cross roads or run on-road, where novice cyclists should be accompanied.

REFRESHMENTS

- Lots of choice in Leicester.
- Cafe in Abbey Park.
- Hope and Anchor pub, Syston.

THINGS TO SEE & DO

- **Blaby Oaks, Blaby:** 2,000 oaks grown from locally collected seed; small pond/ wetland area and a series of circular paths; 01476 581135; www. woodlandtrust.org.uk
- **Jewry Wall Museum:** rare example of surviving Roman city walls; the adjacent museum tells the story of Leicester from prehistory to medieval times; 0116 225 4971; www.visitleicester.co. uk
- **The Guildhall:** well-preserved

timber-framed medieval hall,
now a performance venue and museum;
0116 253 2569;
www.visitleicester.co.uk

- **Abbey Park:** laid out by the Victorians to incorporate the ruins of a 12th-century abbey and its grounds and 17th-century Cavendish House; 0116 222 1000; www.visitleicester.co.uk
- **National Space Centre:** award-winning museum with over 150 interactive experiences, including a ride in the 42m (138ft) high Rocket Tower; 0116 261 0261; www.spacecentre.co.uk
- **Museum of Science & Technology:** evokes 200 years of applied science from early steam to the out-of-this-world technology of today; 0116 299 5111; www.visitleicester.co.uk
- **Watermead Country Park:** a 2-mile (3km) long wildlife haven with many lakes and ponds and a network of rideable paths; 0116 305 5000; www.leics.gov.uk

TRAIN STATIONS
Narborough; South Wigston; Leicester; Syston.

BIKE HIRE
None locally.

FURTHER INFORMATION
- To view or print National Cycle Network routes, visit www.sustrans.org.uk
- Maps for this area are available to buy from www.sustransshop.co.uk
- Spokes (Leicester-based cycling group): 0116 254 8751; www.leicesterspokes.org.uk
- Leicester Tourist Information: 0844 888 5181; www.visitleicester.co.uk

ROUTE DESCRIPTION
Starting from Northfield Park, Blaby, cross Leicester Road and turn right to join National Route 6 to the signalled bypass crossing. Turn left onto Winchester Avenue, then right towards

Town Square,
Leicester

Leicester at the blue Guthlaxton Trail sign. Follow the bridleway to Glen Parva and climb sharply up Cork Lane. Go left at Needham Drive, then right onto Great Central Way, which will take you close to the heart of Leicester. Stay with Route 6 through three sets of traffic signals, which take you over Upperton Road, Western Boulevard and St Augustine Road respectively, to reach Richard III Road near West Bridge.

At the northern end of Richard III Road, a short cycle track leads to rough cobbles (Soar Lane), where you turn right over the river. The signals at the complex Highcross Street junction lead briefly into Sanvey Gate.

Almost immediately, dive left into an alley leading to a maze of quiet business streets. Bear right, turn left at Craven Street, then

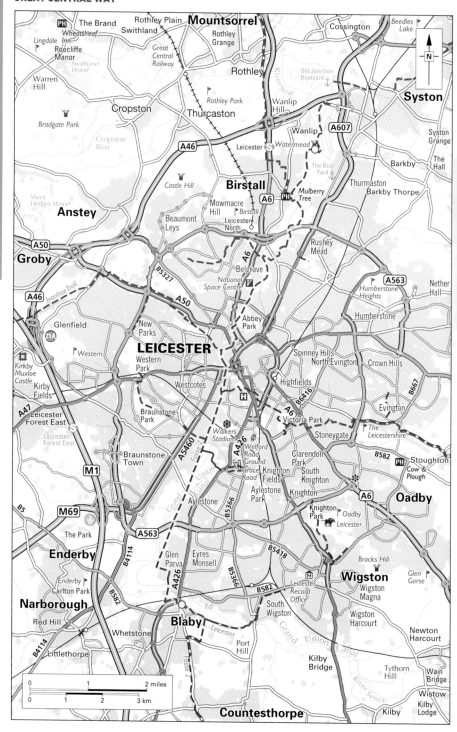

National Space Centre, Leicester

'Woolly Mammoth' by Daniel Fraser Jones

quickly right again onto the footpath along the top edge of Friday Street underpass wall. At St Margaret's Way, turn left onto the cycle track, then right below the road with the River Soar to your left. Go left over the Soar on a concrete footbridge, then right, through a gateway into Abbey Park.

Now you've reached the riverside proper. Enjoy the park itself before crossing Abbey Park Road, heading for the National Space Centre and onwards as far as Thurcaston Road. Turn right over the Soar again, bend round to the left, then go straight over Loughborough Road at the traffic lights.

Bath Street is shut midway to cars but cyclists can easily get past the shrubby roadblock. Where Bath Street veers to the right, before becoming Lanesborough Road, take a left and go off-road again. Follow the track back to the riverside, where you turn right. From here, the path bends a little away from the Soar before joining it again below Watermead Way. Now turn right into Watermead Park following the Route 48 signs and get lost to your heart's content. But watch out for the big Millennium Mammoth!

NEARBY CYCLE ROUTES

From Watermead Park, National Route 6 goes northwards to Loughborough and Derby. From Blaby, it runs south to Market Harborough and Northampton.

Route 63 runs with Route 6 for a short distance. At Bede Park (between Upperton Road and Western Boulevard), it heads east to Oakham and Rutland Water. At Soar Lane (the rough cobbles noted above in the route description), it uses some of the line of the early Swannington railway to reach the National Forest via Glenfield, Ratby and Thornton.

LICHFIELD CITY TO BURTON UPON TRENT

This ride is varied in both the terrain and the visual landscape. Starting in Lichfield, the home town of the 18th-century writer Samuel Johnson, it follows a route through the glorious Staffordshire countryside to Burton upon Trent.

Lichfield has a magnificent cathedral, the relaxing Minster Pool and the traditional Beacon Park to visit. The cathedral is a truly fascinating place and a jewel of this route. There are also two historic houses in the cathedral precinct: the Erasmus Darwin House and Vicar's Close.

On the way to the very attractive town of Burton upon Trent, the route follows the Trent & Mersey Canal. It passes very close to both Fradley Junction, with its award-winning nature reserve, and Alrewas, with the National Memorial Arboretum.

ROUTE INFORMATION
National Routes: 54, 5
Start: Lichfield City train station.
Finish: Burton upon Trent train station.
Distance: 16 miles (26km).
Grade: Medium.
Surface: Tarmac roads.
Hills: Gently rolling hills.

YOUNG & INEXPERIENCED CYCLISTS
A mix of quiet on-road country lanes and traffic-free sections.

REFRESHMENTS
• Lots of choice in Lichfield and Burton upon Trent.
• A number of options in Alrewas.
• Cafe at the National Memorial Arboretum, Alrewas.

THINGS TO SEE & DO
Lichfield:
• Samuel Johnson Birthplace Museum: Grade I listed building, with a variety of displays, reconstructed rooms and audio-visual media; 01543 264972; www.samueljohnsonbirthplace.org.uk
• Lichfield Cathedral: a place of worship for over 1,300 years and the only medieval cathedral in Britain with three spires; the tranquil gardens of Minster Pool are alongside; 01543 306100;

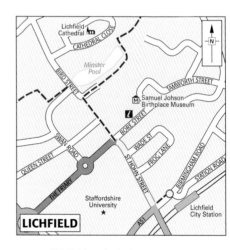

LICHFIELD

www.lichfield-cathedral.org
• Erasmus Darwin House: museum dedicated to the grandfather of Charles Darwin and one of the greatest polymaths of the 17th century; 01543 306260; www.erasmusdarwin.org
• Beacon Park: 100 acres of beautiful formal gardens, open space and leisure facilities; www.lichfielddc.gov.uk
• Chasewater Country Park: 890 acres between Lichfield and Cannock, with opportunities for water-skiing, sailing, angling, bird-watching, rambling and cycling; www.lichfielddc.gov.uk
• Fradley Junction Nature Reserve: woodland paths, bird hides and a towpath encircling

BURTON UPON TRENT

Westgate and Lichfield Cathedral

the reservoir; cafe and visitor centre; 01283 790236; www.waterscape.com
* **National Memorial Arboretum, Alrewas:** memorial honouring armed forces who have died while on duty since World War II; 01283 792333; www.thenma.org.uk

Burton upon Trent:
* **Claymills Victorian Pumping Station, Stretton:** outstanding Victorian industrial monument, with steam engines, beam engines and boilers galore; 01285 509929; www.claymills.org.uk
* **Marston's Brewery:** join the brewery tour to see time-honoured brewing methods in action and enjoy a pint of famous Pedigree bitter; 01902 711811; www.marstons.co.uk
* **The National Forest:** 200 square miles (518 sq km) of new forest in central England already planted with more than 7 million trees; 01283 551211; www.nationalforest.org
* **Branston Water Park:** Green Flag award-winning 40-acre lake surrounded by woodland, wetland and wildflower meadow, supporting a rich variety of bird and wildlife; 01283 508573; www.nationalforest.org

TRAIN STATIONS
Lichfield City; Burton upon Trent.

BIKE HIRE
* **Rosliston Forestry Centre, Rosliston:** 01283 563483; www.roslistonforestrycentre.co.uk

FURTHER INFORMATION
* To view or print National Cycle Network routes, visit www.sustrans.org.uk
* Maps for this area are available to buy from www.sustransshop.co.uk
* **Lichfield Tourist Information:** 01543 412112; www.visitlichfield.co.uk
* **Burton upon Trent Tourist Information:** 01283 508000; www.enjoystaffordshire.co.uk

ROUTE DESCRIPTION
Leave Lichfield City station, cross the road and turn left. Follow the shared-use path along Birmingham Road. At the first signal-controlled

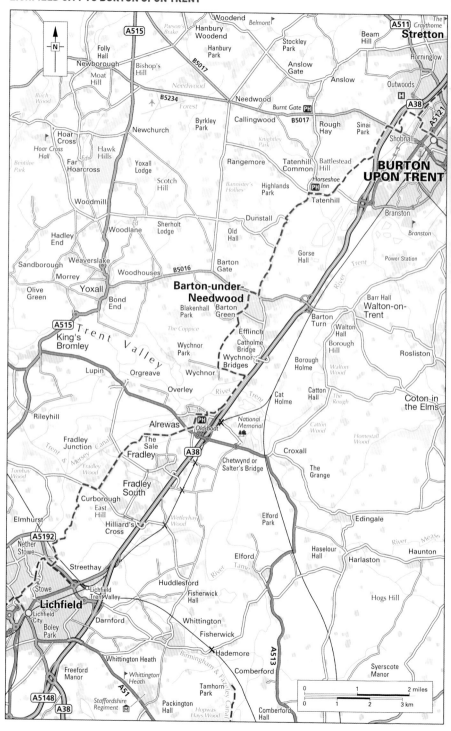

Burton upon Trent
Town Hall

Ferry Bridge over
the River Trent

junction, rejoin the highway and turn right onto St John Street, which leads directly to National Route 54 straight ahead, through a traffic-calmed street. The signs say Route 5 for a spell, until Route 54 is signposted. Turn right after the pedestrian route sign. Cross through a car park, heading to the left of the toilets. The ride branches right onto a traffic-free path alongside Stowe Pool. Follow the signs through the outskirts of Lichfield and onto quiet rural roads with lovely views.

Follow the route for 3 miles (5km) and cross over the canal on a humpback bridge at the road junction. You can visit Fradley Junction by taking the canal towpath. Route 54 winds its way through Alrewas on well-signed quiet roads. The link to the Arboretum is only 1.5 miles (2.5km) from here; it's on a busy main road so take care. Leave the village and join a shared-use path adjacent to the A38 for about a mile (1.6km). Make sure you follow the right sign. The route leaves the path along the A38 after a mile (1.6km) by turning left over the canal. You then continue to Burton upon Trent on a mix of quiet country lanes and a lovely off-road route from Tatenhill, adjacent to Sinai Park, and then directly into the town.

In Burton upon Trent, turn right to follow the route to the Marston's Brewery Shop, then go left into the expansive Shobnall Park. Cross over the canal and follow onwards into the town centre by turning right into Grange Street. After 200m (220 yds), turn left into St Paul's Street West and follow this directly past the Town Hall and around St Paul's Square. On reaching the end of King Edward's Place you have two options: follow the one-way system all the way round or, probably the easiest, walk your bike on the pavement some 50m to Borough Road and on to Burton upon Trent station.

NEARBY CYCLE ROUTES

National Route 54 goes south to Dudley, via Walsall, and north to Derby and Long Eaton.

The National Forest has many cycle routes, from quiet country roads to purpose-designed cycleways (www.nationalforest.org).

MOUNTSORREL TO LOUGHBOROUGH & SHEPSHED

Mountsorrel village is situated between the River Soar and the rocky crags of Charnwood Forest. It is a delightful little place, with various local treasures such as the village pump, which was made of local granite and erected to commemorate Queen Victoria's Golden Jubilee. In the Castle Gardens is a stone statue of a knight; the work of local sculptor Mike Grevatte. The Butter Market was erected in 1793 to protect stallholders from the weather and to replace the original medieval market cross, which is now sited at Swithland. The red-brick bridge was built in 1860 to carry granite over the river. With its span of 27m (89ft), it is still one of the largest brick arches in the country. The Waterside Inn has sat on the edge of Mountsorrel Lock since 1795. The Castle Hill is a registered Ancient Monument – Mountsorrel Castle was destroyed in 1217. If you make it to the top of the steep and rocky climb, there is a good view across the Soar Valley to the east.

Loughborough is famed for its university and colleges, and has a unique atmosphere and wealth of historic buildings. The Italianate Town Hall was originally built as the town's Corn Exchange in 1855. The oldest edifice in Market Square is the drinking fountain, financed by Archdeacon Henry Fearon in 1870, when Loughborough gained its first piped water supply.

In 1997, the Market Square gained a controversial, but award-winning, contemporary sculpture by Shona Kinloch. *The Sock* celebrates the woollen and hosiery industries, so vital in Loughborough's early industrial development.

Boats on the River Soar

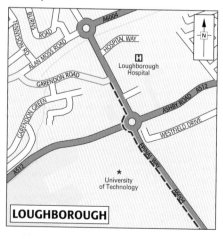

LOUGHBOROUGH

ROUTE INFORMATION
National Route: 6
Start: Cafe at Stonehurst Family Farm,
Mountsorrel.
Finish: Market Place, Shepshed.
Distance: 8 miles (13km). Longer option: from
Stonehurst Family Farm, Mountsorrel, to
Shepshed and returning to Loughborough
12 miles (19km).
Grade: Easy.
Surface: On-road from Mountsorrel to the
outskirts of Loughborough, then a shared-use
cyclepath to Shepshed.
Hills: Flat, with no significant hills.

YOUNG & INEXPERIENCED CYCLISTS
Suitable for older, more competent children
and adult novices.

REFRESHMENTS
- A number of options in Mountsorrel,
  including the Waterside Inn and Swan pubs.
- Lots of choice in Quorn.
- Lots of choice in Loughborough.
- The Railway Hotel pub, Shepshed.

THINGS TO SEE & DO
- **Stonehurst Family Farm & Museum,
  Mountsorrel:** all the animals of a working

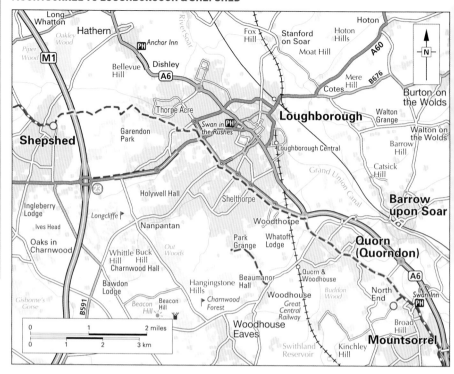

farm, motor museum, farm shop and cafe; 01509 413216; www.stonehurstfarm.co.uk
- **Mountsorrel Castle:** 11th-century earthwork motte-and-bailey fortress; 0116 230 3809; www.mountsorrel.org.uk

Loughborough:
- **Great Central Railway:** mainline heritage railway, travelling from Loughborough to Leicester; considered one of the greatest railway journeys in the world; 01509 632323; www.gcrailway.co.uk
- **Charnwood Museum:** permanent exhibition exploring the area, both past and present; includes an extensive collection of Ladybird children's books; within Queen's Park; 01509 233754; www.leics.gov.uk
- **Queen's Park:** Green Flag park, with bowling green, bandstand, aviaries, maze, Carillon Tower War Memorial and Museum; 01509 634975; www.charnwood.gov.uk
- **Taylor's Bell Foundry:** where the Big Ben bell was made; museum and shop; 01509 212241; www.taylorbells.co.uk

- **Garendon Park, Loughborough:** ancient religious settlement; www.charnwood.gov.uk

TRAIN STATIONS
Sileby; Barrow upon Soar; Loughborough.

BIKE HIRE
None locally.

FURTHER INFORMATION
- To view or print National Cycle Network routes, visit www.sustrans.org.uk
- Maps for this area are available to buy from www.sustransshop.co.uk
- **Mountsorrel Tourist Information:** 0116 230 3809; www.mountsorrel.org.uk
- **Loughborough Tourist Information:** 01509 218113; www.charnwood.gov.uk
- **Leicestershire Tourist Information:** 0844 888 5181; www.goleicestershire.com
- Visit www.leics.gov.uk/charnwood_cycle_map.pdf for details of how to get from Route 6 to Loughborough train station.

Beacon Hill in autumn

ROUTE DESCRIPTION

Leave the cafe at Stonehurst Family Farm in Mountsorrel and turn left out of the car park onto Bond Lane. Follow this to the T-junction with Loughborough Road. This is National Route 6. Turn left here and follow the signs to Loughborough. If you want to visit the Great Central Railway, after passing through Quorn turn left at the only set of traffic lights in the village and follow this road for half a mile (0.8km) to Quorn & Woodhouse station.

Back on the route, follow Route 6 along William Davis Way over the railway – this is a good place to see trains steaming into and out of Loughborough. Before reaching the university campus, you can branch off right from the route into the town centre. Otherwise continue through the campus to where the route turns off left. This takes you along quiet back streets to Garendon Road. Follow the signs until you find the lovely traffic-free route through Garendon Park. From here it is easy riding to Shepshed.

When you leave the traffic-free route at Shepshed Football Club, you have the choice of finishing your ride in Shepshed by turning right and going downhill to the Market Place, or turning left to follow the cycle route back to Loughborough.

NEARBY CYCLE ROUTES

National Route 6 goes northwards from Loughborough to Derby, Nottingham and Sheffield. To the south, it goes to Market Harborough, Northampton, Milton Keynes and Leighton Buzzard.

'The Sock' sculpture, Loughborough

77

ASHBY WOULDS HERITAGE TRAIL

For centuries, coal lay at the heart of this part of the Leicestershire/Derbyshire borderlands. However, the area now falls within the new National Forest, and the ex-industrial landscape has changed spectacularly since its foundation in 1990. Ravaged mining scenes are being comprehensively supplanted by new woodland and community life as the 200 square mile (518sq km) forest vision grows by the year.

Ashby Woulds Heritage Trail follows the old Ashby & Nuneaton Railway, which opened in 1873 and replaced an 18th-century canal. The trail runs from Measham to the edge of Swadlincote, passing through countryside rich in social and industrial history.

At Moira, you can stop off at Conkers, a forest-themed visitor centre, with a wide range of indoor and outdoor activities, including a little railway and an indoor adventure playground. Close by, at Waterside, the northern basin of the Ashby Canal has been rebuilt from scratch. The canal was closed by subsidence in the 1940s but is slowly being filled with water, drop by drop. Eventually, it will reconnect with the national canal network at Snarestone, south of Measham. You can already ride the towpath, snaking back to rejoin the Heritage Trail via Moira Furnace, thought to be the best-preserved 19th-century blast furnace in Europe.

ROUTE INFORMATION

National Route: 63
Start: Measham Library, High Street, Measham.
Finish: Thorpe Downs Road, Church Gresley.
Distance: 5 miles (8km). Longer option via Moira Furnace 6 miles (9.5km).

Grade: Easy.
Surface: Railway path.
Hills: Largely flat with ramped links.

YOUNG & INEXPERIENCED CYCLISTS

Mostly traffic-free, so ideal for novice cyclists

Cycling along Ashby Canal towpath

and families. Care is needed at a couple of road crossings.

REFRESHMENTS
- Pubs along the route.
- Cafes at Moira Furnace and Conkers.
- Picnic areas at Conkers.
- Lots of choice in Swadlincote.

THINGS TO SEE & DO
- Moira Furnace, Swadlincote: early 19th-century iron-making furnace, with displays and stories about former inhabitants, lime kilns, craft shops, tearoom, boat trips, play area; 01283 224667; www.nwleicestershire.gov.uk
- Sarah's Wood, close to Conkers: 24-acre site in the National Forest, which has been transformed into a woodland wildlife haven, with a play area designed for children with special needs; 0116 265 7061; www.nationalforest.org
- Willesley Wood: award-winning woodland and one of the first woods to evolve within Leicestershire's former coalfield; new and

mature woods, wetlands, wildflower meadows and the rare majestic black poplar, plus over 70 different types of bird; 01476 581135; www.woodlandtrust.org.uk
- Conkers Visitor Centre and Waterside: over 120 acres of grounds, with sculpture trails, assault course and adventure playground; train ride to the events area, where there are restaurant facilities and cycle parking; 01283 216633; www.visitconkers.com

TRAIN STATIONS
None.

BIKE HIRE
- Just Bikes, Moira Furnace: 01530 415021; www.justbikesashby.com

FURTHER INFORMATION
- To view or print National Cycle Network routes, visit www.sustrans.org.uk
- Maps for this area are available to buy from www.sustransshop.co.uk
- National Forest: 01283 551211; www.nationalforest.org

Moira Furnace on the
Ashby Canal

- Ashby-de-la-Zouch Tourist Information:
  01530 411767; www.nwleics.gov.uk

ROUTE DESCRIPTION

Following NCN63 signs, notice Anne-Marie
Scott's colourful timber town sign beside
Measham Library before heading up the ramp
to the old railway trail. Turn right. The way soon
ducks under the A42 by weaving left, running
briefly alongside a local road, then dodging
back up onto its historic line. Next is an open
country section, with a link to the old mining
village of Oakthorpe and a ramped climb to
Church Road, Donisthorpe, crossed over speed

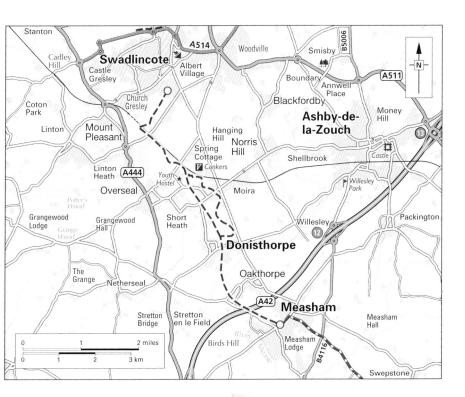

bumps. Enter the old Donisthorpe Colliery site, now a woodland park, where several side links include an alternative route past Moira Furnace. Having skirted Moira on a high embankment, the trail broadens out into a nature reserve, once home to hundreds of railway coal wagons, gathered here before dispersing on their migrations. Watch out for right forks towards Waterside and Conkers Visitor Centre. Pass one of Britain's newest youth hostels on your left before reaching Spring Cottage Road, close by the Navigation pub. Take great care at the road crossing here and also about half a mile (0.8km) further on, at Park Road. Now you ride into deep woodland on a serpentine course that veers generally to the right. After several side turns to the left and right, head for Church Gresley and Albert Village, ending in Thorpe Downs Road.

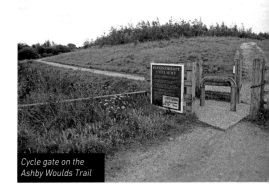

Cycle gate on the Ashby Woulds Trail

NEARBY CYCLE ROUTES

Beyond Measham, National Route 63 follows country roads across Leicestershire and through the centre of Leicester to reach Oakham and Rutland Water.

DERBY CANAL PATH & THE CLOUD TRAIL

The route out of Derby to Worthington was one of the first built by Sustrans. It starts near the heart of the city and sets out on an attractive path beside the River Derwent, which would take you to Elvaston Castle if you wished. However, the Canal Path turns south away from the river and follows the course of a dry waterway to join the still navigable Trent & Mersey Canal at Swarkestone. After about 1 mile (1.6km), you leave the towpath to join the Cloud Trail, a dismantled railway path that will take you as far as the village of Worthington and up to nearby Cloud Quarry. On the way, watch out for colourful milemarkers and four enigmatic wayside figures made of Swithland slate.

The Derby Canal Path and the Cloud Trail are part of the much longer Route 6 of the National Cycle Network, which runs all the way from London to the Lake District.

Melbourne is an appealing town just off the route, with thatched, whitewashed cottages and the remains of a 14th-century castle. Just beyond Melbourne, you will see the outline of the Norman church of St Mary and St Hardulph set high on the limestone bluff above the village of Breedon on the Hill.

ROUTE INFORMATION

National Route: 6
Start: Derby train station or the Riverside Path in the centre of Derby (Bass's Recreation Ground).
Finish: Worthington and Cloud Quarry.
Distance: 13 miles (21km).
Grade: Easy.
Surface: Traffic-free, fine-quality stone paths with short road sections.
Hills: None.

YOUNG & INEXPERIENCED CYCLISTS

Once onto the Riverside Path, the route is excellent for novices and young children. All the busy roads are crossed via bridges, subways or toucan crossings. There is a 1-mile (1.6km) road section to visit Melbourne and a shorter, quieter road section to visit Worthington.

View across Melbourne Lake

REFRESHMENTS
- Lots of choice in Derby.
- Lots of choice in Melbourne.
- Malt Shovel pub in Worthington.

THINGS TO SEE & DO

Derby:
- **Derby Cathedral:** from the station, follow Route 6 in the other direction towards the city centre; 01332 341201; www.derbycathedral.org
- **Derby Museum and Art Gallery;** 01332 641901; www.derby.gov.uk
- **Silk Mill:** one of the first factories in the UK and part of the Derwent Valley Mills World Heritage Site; 01332 255308; www.derby.gov.uk
- **Swarkestone:** village where Bonnie Prince Charlie turned his army around in 1745, making it the southernmost point reached by the army on its way to London. Swarkestone Bridge was built in the 14th century.
- **Trent Viaduct, near Melbourne:** Grade II listed structure, built in 1869 and repaired by Sustrans in the late 1980s.

Cloud Cuckoos sculpture

- **Melbourne:** remains of a 14th-century castle.
- **The Cloud Cuckoos:** a pair of giant iron birds fiercely guard their only egg, close to the edge of Cloud Quarry.
- **Worthington:** village boasting an attractive church with a small wooden spire and an octagonal red-brick lock-up dating back to the 18th century.

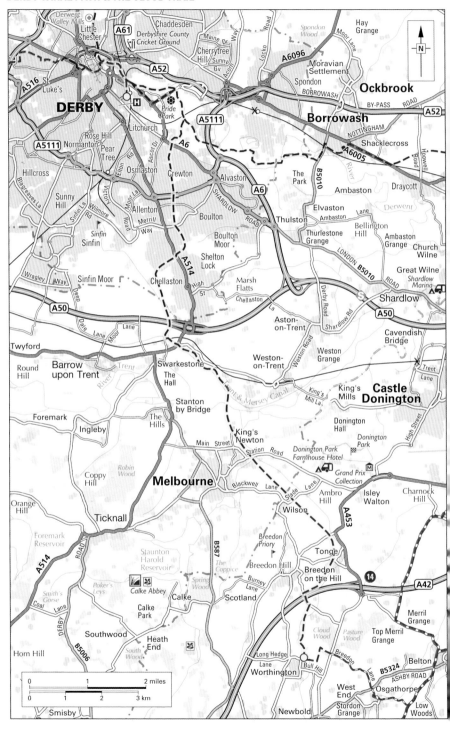

Breedon on the Hill
church and cliff

TRAIN STATIONS
Derby.

BIKE HIRE
Enquire locally.

FURTHER INFORMATION
- To view or print National Cycle Network routes, visit www.sustrans.org.uk
- Maps for this area are available to buy from www.sustransshop.co.uk
- Derby Tourist Information: 01332 255802; www.visitderby.co.uk

ROUTE DESCRIPTION
Starting at Derby train station (Pride Park exit), use the link route to join the Riverside Path. Follow this eastbound for about 1.5 miles (2.5km) before turning south onto Derby Canal Path, a specially built cyclepath that takes you to the Trent & Mersey Canal at Swarkestone. Turn left onto the towpath then, after another mile (1.6km), turn right, leaving the towpath to join the Cloud Trail. This traffic-free path crosses the Trent Viaduct near Melbourne, then skirts the villages of King's Newton and Wilson en route to Worthington.

Watch out for a left turn, just before Worthington car park. Ride around and up to the rim of Cloud Quarry, which has dramatic viewpoints and the sardonic *Cloud Cuckoos*.

From the Cuckoos, it's possible to continue along quiet lanes and traffic-free sections for 10 miles (16km) to Loughborough, where there is a train station. Follow the signs for Route 6.

NEARBY CYCLE ROUTES
Derby is at a major junction of the National Cycle Network and has more than its share of associated traffic-free paths.

Derby Riverside Path follows the Derwent east to a turn-off for Elvaston Castle Country Park, with its tearoom and perimeter track. Beyond Elvaston Route 6 leads, partly off-road, via Borrowash and Breaston to Long Eaton.

To the north of Derby city centre (Exeter Bridge), National Route 54 enters the Derwent Valley Mills World Heritage Site, brushing past the Silk Mill Industrial Museum and on to Chester Green and Darley Abbey.

About 1.5 miles (2.5km) west of the city centre, the other arm of National Route 54 joins a largely traffic-free trail that runs 6 miles (9.5km) to Hilton.

For a more ambitious ride, take the National Route 68 turn at Etwall. From here, join the Pennine Cycleway, which takes you up hill and down dale, all the way to the Scottish border.

NUTBROOK TRAIL

This varied and largely traffic-free route starts out along the Erewash Canal before diverting onto an old railway line through diverse landscapes of homely suburbs, hedged fields, industrial archaeology and 'urban fallow'.

The Miller-Mundy family developed Shipley in the 18th century as a country estate and a coal-mining area, building a feeder canal to take their coal down the Nutbrook Valley to join the main Erewash Canal. Then began a period of dramatic change as the railway supplanted the local canal, Stanton steelworks mushroomed and towns sprang up to house the workers employed in all the new industries.

The M1 motorway arrived in the mid-20th century, old industries declined and reclamation of the landscapes of muck and brass began. Now, at Shipley Country Park, Derbyshire County Council has converted rails to trails, graded and seeded old stockpiles and planted over half a million trees. Nature has restocked its woods and wetlands, and the visitor centre has become a popular meeting place, complete with a secure toddlers' playground.

Nearby Trent lock on the Erewash Canal

ROUTE INFORMATION

National Route: 67
Start: Royal Avenue, Long Eaton.
Finish: Shipley Country Park.
Distance: 9 miles (14.5km).
Longer option: from Long Eaton to Heanor 10.5 miles (17km).
Grade: Easy.
Surface: Varied but mostly tarmac trails.
Hills: A few. See route description.

YOUNG & INEXPERIENCED CYCLISTS

The Nutbrook Trail is ideal for novice cyclists and families, although there is a bit of a climb in the middle of Shipley Country Park and another climb near Heanor.

REFRESHMENTS

- Lots of choice in Long Eaton and Ilkeston.
- Old Black Horse pub, Mapperley.
- Cafe in the visitor centre at Shipley Country Park.

THINGS TO SEE & DO

- Lock Lane Ash Tip, near Long Eaton: valuable habitat for a variety of wildlife,

with more than 200 species of moth and 16 species of butterfly; 01773 881188; www.derbyshirewildlifetrust.org.uk
- **Erewash Museum, Ilkeston:** tells the unique history of the Erewash area; 0115 907 1141; www.erewashmuseum.co.uk
- **Mapperley Wood:** nature reserve, with a narrow belt of woodland and a stream; contains some of the county's most vulnerable habitats; permit needed to access the bird hides; 01773 881188; www.derbyshirewildlifetrust.org.uk

- **Shipley Country Park:** 600 acres of varied landscape; 18 miles (29km) of footpaths, with lakes, trails, an abundance of wildlife, a sculpture trail and an adventure playground; 01773 719961; www.derbyshire.gov.uk

TRAIN STATIONS
Long Eaton.

BIKE HIRE
- **Shipley Country Park:** 01773 719961; www.peakdistrictonline.co.uk

NUTBROOK TRAIL

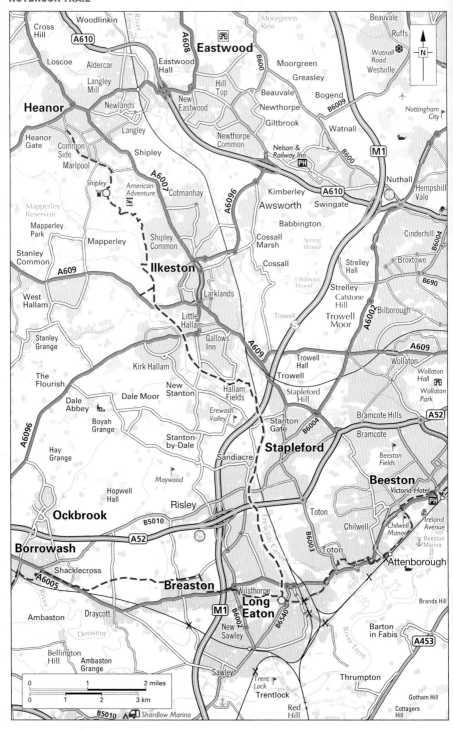

A Victorian kitchen, Erewash Museum

FURTHER INFORMATION

- To view or print National Cycle Network routes, visit www.sustrans.org.uk
- Maps for this area are available to buy from www.sustransshop.co.uk
- Derbyshire Tourist Information: 0845 833 0970; www.visitpeakdistrict.com

ROUTE DESCRIPTION

Start in Long Eaton at the end of Royal Avenue, where National Route 67 is clearly signposted. The trail proper starts out across the Erewash flood meadows alongside what was once one of Britain's biggest railway marshalling yards at Toton. Before long, it joins the canal for a few miles before diverting to the left, off the towpath, near the old Stanton ironworks.

Here, you have to watch diligently for the sequence of Route 67 signs, which takes you briefly along a dusty back road redolent of once-vibrant industry. Now you join the railway trail that skirts Kirk Hallam to the left, Ilkeston to the right. Watch for a left turn to Whitefurrows, which will one day become part of Route 672 between Derby and Nottingham.

Next, at Lodge House near Lodge Farm, you turn right towards what used be an adventure park, then go left, up the hill, to Shipley Country Park. To reach Heanor, you can ride westwards

from the park, turn right onto a quiet lane then left onto the bed of the old Great Northern Railway, which takes you on to Thorpe's Road.

NEARBY CYCLE ROUTES

From Long Eaton, you can join National Route 6 to go westwards to Derby. Going in the other direction, you can check out Attenborough Nature Reserve and Nottingham's Big Track (see page 90).

Wildlife abounds on the Nutbrook Trail

NOTTINGHAM'S BIG TRACK

Nottingham's hugely popular Big Track is a circular, traffic-free ride alongside the Nottingham Canal and the River Trent, passing close to several of the city's major venues and attractions. The area is rich with sites of natural and historical interest, and there are many opportunities to vary your route to make the most of them.

Nottingham is not just the fabled home to Robin Hood and Sherwood Forest, it was also the inspiration for literary giants Lord Byron and D. H. Lawrence. It has a varied and fascinating past, from ancient underground caves and a famous lace industry to the turbulent and dramatic history of the castle. Today, Nottingham is a well-balanced blend of the old and the new. Its skyline is dominated by Nottingham Castle – the original castle was burned down during the English Civil War, leaving only the medieval gatehouse, and a fine ducal mansion was built to replace it. Shopping centres such as Broadmarsh are neatly juxtaposed with the Lace Market. Once the heart of the world lace industry, this historic quarter-mile (0.4km) square is a protected heritage area and retains many impressive examples of 18th-century industrial architecture.

ROUTE INFORMATION

National Route: This route is not part of the National Cycle Network.
Start and Finish: Nottingham train station.
Distance: 11 miles (17.5km). Other options: from Nottingham train station to Attenborough Nature Reserve 6 miles (9.5km); from Nottingham train station to Holme Pierrepont 5 miles (8km).
Grade: Easy.
Surface: Gravel.
Hills: Mostly flat but with some steep wheeling ramps.

Newstead Abbey, home to Lord Byron

Statue of Robin Hood, erected in 1952

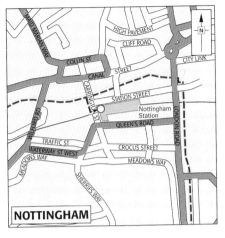

NOTTINGHAM

YOUNG & INEXPERIENCED CYCLISTS

The section from Nottingham station to Beeston is ideal. Otherwise, young and inexperienced cyclists are best accompanied, as the ride runs close to either a canal or a river.

REFRESHMENTS

- Lots of choice in Nottingham.
- Cafe at Attenborough Nature Centre.

THINGS TO SEE & DO

- **Nottingham Castle:** magnificent 17th-century ducal mansion, with spectacular

Nottingham's medieval
Severns building

views across the city, now a vibrant museum
and art gallery; 0115 915 3700;
www.nottinghamcity.gov.uk

- Museum of Nottingham Life, Brewhouse
  Yard, Nottingham: housed in a group of five
  restored 17th-century cottages; offers a
  realistic glimpse of everyday life in
  Nottingham over the past 300 years;
  0115 915 3700; www.nottinghamcity.gov.uk
- Colwick Country Park: 60 acres of parkland,
  with a large and diverse area of water,
  woodland and meadows; rich diversity of
  wildlife and wildfowl; opposite Colwick
  Woods Local Nature Reserve;
  www.nottinghamcity.gov.uk
- Wollaton Hall, Gardens & Deer Park:
  Elizabethan mansion set in spectacular
  gardens and parkland; home to
  Nottingham's Natural History Museum and
  Industrial Museum, and the Yard Gallery;
  0115 915 3900; www.nottinghamcity.gov.uk
- Attenborough Nature Centre: nature
  reserve, with a maze of willow-framed paths,

lakes, bridges, moorings and wildfowl;
educational facilities; 0115 958 8242;
www.attenboroughnaturecentre.co.uk

- Newstead Abbey Historic House & Gardens:
  beautiful historic house, with Lord Byron's
  private apartments; set in over 300 acres of
  gardens and parkland; 01623 455900;
  www.newsteadabbey.org.uk

TRAIN STATIONS
Nottingham; Beeston; Attenborough.

BIKE HIRE
- Bunney's Bikes, Carrington Street:
  0115 947 2713; www.bunneysbikes.com

FURTHER INFORMATION
- To view or print National Cycle Network
  routes, visit www.sustrans.org.uk
- Two free maps (North and South sheets) are
  available from 0115 915 6596
- Further details on the Big Track can be found
  at www.thebigwheel.org.uk

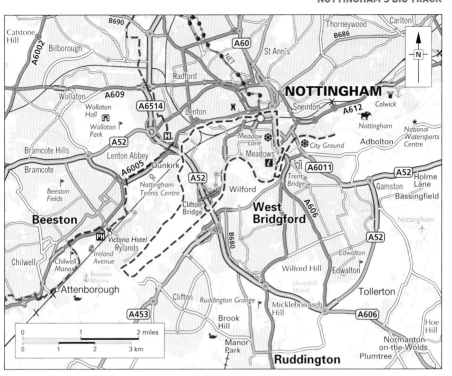

- Nottingham Tourist Information:
0844 477 5678; www.visitnottingham.com

ROUTE DESCRIPTION

Turn right outside Nottingham station, and
push your bike across the Carrington Street
zebra crossing, then go left down onto the canal
promenade. Turn sharp right, doubling back
under Carrington Street, and head off along the
towpath, with the canal on your left. Take extra
care at the blind right-hand bend below London
Road. The towpath leads you to a ramp that
takes you over the canal and all the way to the
River Trent. Bear right on the path, following
the northern side of the Trent, right through the
city and out into the countryside.

Press on upstream, with Clifton Woods above
the far bank on one side and broad, flat fields
on the other. After a mile (1.6km) or so, the
track bends right towards Beeston Weir, where
you have a choice of possible routes.

You could turn right without crossing
Beeston Lock and head back to town, with the

canal on your left. Alternatively, it is well worth
leaving Big Track proper and continuing
southwestwards to Attenborough Nature
Reserve. Take care crossing the narrow
bridges at Beeston Lock and please give way
to pedestrians. Turn left for Beeston Marina,
where there are plenty of places to stop for
refreshments, but please heed the signs asking
cyclists to dismount in this busy area. With the
Trent still on your left, watch for signs in a mile
(1.6km) or so advising a right turn to the
modern visitor centre, or ask someone the way
– you are rarely alone in this willow-fringed
maze of paths and lakes.

NEARBY CYCLE ROUTES

National Route 6 links Nottingham with Derby,
via Beeston and Long Eaton.

Nottingham's own cycle network is also well
worth exploring. 'Rural Rides' is a programme
of guided cycle rides around the city
(www.nottinghamshire.gov.uk/home/
leisure/l-cycling-body/ruralrides.htm)

SILVER HILL & FIVE PITS TRAIL

Forty years ago, this area was a landscape of coal mines. Now that it's extensively reclaimed, walkers, cyclists, horse-riders and wildlife share a cat's cradle of old railways, once ruled by shuffling goods trains. The ride includes part of the old Great Central line, which used to serve the collieries at Grassmoor, Williamthorpe, Holmewood, Pilsley and Tibshelf. It offers a family-friendly route between Teversal in Nottinghamshire and Grassmoor in Derbyshire. It is not fully waymarked, so be sure to collect guides before you start and allow time to explore some of the loops and diversions en route.

Together with the local footpath network, the trails also offer a range of circuit walks, including several local nature reserves, designated to conserve a diversity of creatures, flora and geology.

Teversal has its own local walks, including a Sculpture Trail resulting from an ongoing collaboration between the community and professional artists. Leaflets describing the walks, local wildlife and industrial heritage are available at the Teversal Visitor Centre.

ROUTE INFORMATION
National Route: 67
Start: Teversal Trails Visitor Centre.
Finish: Grassmoor village.
Distance: 8 miles (13km).
Grade: Easy.
Surface: All-weather, mostly rolled stone.
Hills: Mostly gently graded, though steeper where old railway bridges have been removed.

Restored machinery inside Stainsby Mill

YOUNG & INEXPERIENCED CYCLISTS
Mostly traffic-free.

REFRESHMENTS
- Several options in Teversal, including a cafe at Teversal Trails Visitor Centre.
- Several options in Tibshelf and Grassmoor.
- Picnic sites along the way, including at Grassmoor Country Park.

THINGS TO SEE & DO
- **Brierley Forest Park, Sutton in Ashfield:** built on a colliery site; offers trails, recreation facilities, art and sculptures, wildflower meadow, pond and visitor centre; 01623 550172; www.ashfield-dc.gov.uk
- **North Wingfield nature reserve:** refuge for water vole; small oak woodland and surrounding grassland containing many different plant and several butterfly species; 01773 881188; www.derbyshirewildlifetrust.org.uk
- **Holmewood Woodlands:** habitat for many birds; butterflies frequent the grassland, and dragonflies may be seen around the pond in summer; you can wander across farmland to historic Stainsby village, Stainsby Mill and Hardwick Hall; 0845 605 8058; www.derbyshire.gov.uk

Hardwick Hall

- Stainsby Mill, Hardwick Estate: impressive, fully functioning water-powered flour mill and 19th-century water mill; 01246 850430; www.nationaltrust.org.uk
- Hardwick Hall: spectacular Tudor treasure house built for 'Bess of Hardwick', Elizabethan England's second most powerful and wealthy woman; outstanding 16th- and 17th-century tapestries and embroideries, fine historic parkland, orchard and herb garden; 01246 850430; www.nationaltrust.org.uk

TRAIN STATIONS
Chesterfield; Mansfield Woodhouse.

BIKE HIRE
None locally.

FURTHER INFORMATION
- To view or print National Cycle Network routes, visit www.sustrans.org.uk
- Free maps for this area are available from Nottingham County Council; 08449 808080; www.nottscc.gov.uk
- Derbyshire Tourist Information: 0845 833 0970; www.visitpeakdistrict.com
- Mansfield Tourist Information: 01623 463463; www.mansfield.gov.uk
- Teversal Trails: 01623 442021; www.teversaltrails.com

ROUTE DESCRIPTION
You'll find Teversal Trails Visitor Centre at the end of Carnarvon Street, off the B6014 near Teversal. Ride past the Coal Garden, go left and left again to join Silverhill Greenway, which

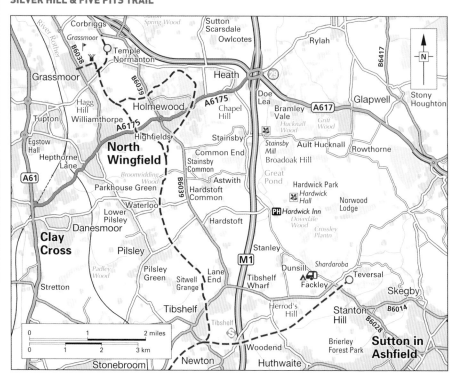

The white track of the Five Pits Trail

runs southwestwards towards Tibshelf through wooded cuttings or between tall hedges for about 3 miles (5km). After diving below the M1, watch out for a junction where you turn off to the right through a steel gateway to join Five Pits Trail.

Tibshelf Ponds, once a colliery, is now a fine landscape of meadows and woodland, displaying little trace of its mining past. In Tibshelf, you'll find shops, pubs and a church before riding the big dipper down across a broad, open valley and up the other side towards Hardstoft. Now on the line of the old Great Central, the trail sweeps on, sometimes with wide west views over rolling countryside to the Peak District, sometimes threading through dark areas of forest and ex-industrial villages.

Beyond Timber Lane Picnic Site, you face a choice: to the left, the main route veers towards Highfields and Grassmoor; to the right, you turn into Holmewood Loop, which, although mostly off-road, is a maze of turns and cross trails, best navigated with the help of the Five Pits Trail pamphlet and a good sense of direction.

Although the main off-road trail will one day reach Chesterfield, it presently ends at the village of Grassmoor, where you'll find pubs and a shop.

NEARBY CYCLE ROUTES
From Teversal Visitor Centre, Teversal Trail heads eastwards towards Skegby, then north to Pleasley. If you've time and a map, ask the way to the A617 underpass leading to Meden Trail and the former Viyella woollen mills, set deep in the limestone gorge of Pleasley Vale.

In and around Chesterfield, you'll find more rides, including the Hipper Valley and Holmewood Greenways and part of the Trans Pennine Trail, which heads northwards on the Chesterfield Canal (also National Route 67) to Killamarsh.

THE MANIFOLD TRAIL – STAFFORDSHIRE

The Manifold Valley winds its way through some of the most spectacular scenery in the Peak District National Park. It follows the route made for the Leek & Manifold Valley Light Railway up the valleys of the Hamps and Manifold rivers, both of which run underground for part of their courses. The railway opened in 1904 and closed 30 years later to become one of Britain's first ever railway trails. Some of the limestone landscapes through which it passes have been classified as Sites of Special Scientific Interest (SSSIs), providing habitat for a wide range of species. Watch out for kingfishers and even otters.

  Thor's Cave is the most spectacular sight of the Manifold Valley, a 10m (33ft) opening, high in a tooth-like rock, in which ancient stone tools and the remains of now-extinct animals have been found. Swainsley Tunnel was built to spare the owners of Swainsley Hall the sound and sight of the trains. At Hulme End, you'll find picnic seats, a static model railway, and toilets at the visitor centre, as well as a shop and pub in the village.

Thor's Cave,
Manifold Valley

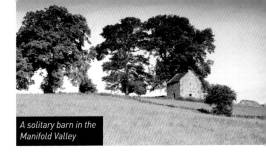
A solitary barn in the Manifold Valley

ROUTE INFORMATION

National Route: 54
Start: Waterhouses old station car park.
Finish: Visitor Centre, Hulme End.
Distance: 8 miles (13km).
Grade: Easy.
Surface: Some stone, some tarmac.
Hills: No serious hills.

YOUNG & INEXPERIENCED CYCLISTS

Well-surfaced track with gentle gradients.
Traffic-free apart from one 2-mile (3km)
on-lane section from Wetton Mill to Swainsley
Tunnel. Take care crossing the A523.

REFRESHMENTS

- Several options in or near Waterhouses.
- Cafe at Wetton Mill.
- The Manifold Inn, Hulme End.

THINGS TO SEE & DO

- Ilam Park and South Peak Estate: east of
  Waterhouses; beautiful country park running
  along both banks of the River Manifold;

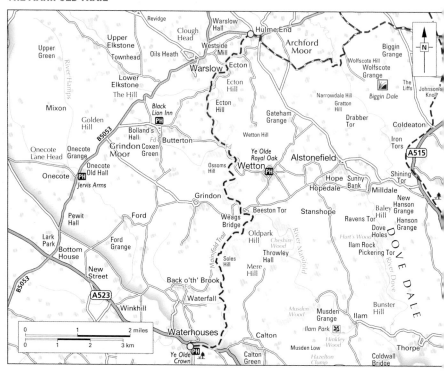

spectacular views towards Dovedale; visitor centre, tearoom and shop; 01335 350503; www.nationaltrust.org.uk

- **Thor's Cave, near Wetton:** the most spectacular sight of the Manifold Valley; inhabited over 10,000 years ago; www.cressbrook.co.uk
- **Wetton Mill, Wetton:** redundant corn mill that closed in 1857; now converted into a scenic picnic spot, tearoom and two National Trust holiday cottages; 01335 350503; www.nationaltrust.org.uk
- **Weag's Barn, near Grindon:** 45 acres of meadow, grassland and valley woodland; internationally important for the wildlife that it supports; 01889 880100; www.staffs-wildlife.org.uk
- **Castern Wood, south of Wetton:** 50 acres of ancient woodland and species-rich limestone grassland, with unrivalled views across the Manifold Valley; 01889 880100; www.staffs-wildlife.org.uk
- **Blackbrook Zoological Park, Winkhill:** set

amid the Staffordshire Moorlands; large collection of rare and endangered species; 01538 308293; www.blackbrookzoo.co.uk

TRAIN STATIONS
None.

BIKE HIRE
- **Brown End Farm Cycle Hire, Waterhouses:** 01538 308313; www.manifoldcycling-brownendfarm.co.uk
- **Manifold Valley Cycle Hire:** 01538 308609; www.visitpeakdistrict.com

FURTHER INFORMATION
- To view or print National Cycle Network routes, visit www.sustrans.org.uk
- Maps for this area are available to buy from www.sustransshop.co.uk
- **Manifold Valley Tourist Information:** 01298 84679; www.peakdistrict.nationaltrust.org.uk
- **Leek Tourist Information:** 01538 483741; www.staffsmoorlands.gov.uk

The entrance to Thor's Cave

ROUTE DESCRIPTION

The route is well used by walkers and dogs, and becomes quite crowded on peak days in summer. Please ride with care and regard for all others you meet along the way.

Start out from what was Waterhouses station, just south of the A523, along the traffic-free track at the back of the car park heading east. You soon reach the A523 crossing where particular care is needed. From here, the path joins the steep-sided valley of the River Hamps as it winds northwards.

Just below Beeston Tor, you join the River Manifold, then pass below Thor's Cave. This was occupied by Paleolithic hunter-gatherers over 10,000 years ago and, though high above the trail, the scramble up is well worth the effort to explore inside or to admire the excellent views. From the cave, a footpath leads walkers to the village of Wetton.

Back on the trail, a 2-mile (3km) section from Wetton Mill to Swainsley Tunnel is shared with light motor traffic. The Tunnel is narrow and care is needed, although it is illuminated and runs in a straight line so that you can see drivers and they can see you quite well.

The last 1.5 miles (2.5km) runs through more open countryside to Hulme End.

NEARBY CYCLE ROUTES

Making loops from the Manifold Trail is relatively easy for map-readers. Steep on-lane options might take in Butterton, Grindon or Ford to the west, or Wetton to the east. However, if you do pick your own route, it's best to stay well away from the A523.

TISSINGTON & HIGH PEAK TRAILS

These two trails are the most famous railway paths in the Peak District, passing through neat pastures bounded by drystone walls and the dramatic limestone scenery of the Derbyshire Dales, including several rock cuttings. The two trails link at Parsley Hay. On the Tissington Trail, there is a steady climb of almost 213m (700ft) from Ashbourne to Parsley Hay. For this reason, it is worth starting at Ashbourne when you are fresh, going uphill towards Parsley Hay, leaving you with a downhill ride on the way back.

The High Peak Trail offers a superb challenge in the heart of the Peak District, from High Peak Junction via Middleton Top and Parsley Hay to Sparklow. This ride describes the section from Middleton Top to Parsley Hay. Following it in this direction means that you have an uphill climb on the outward journey and downhill on the return. Unless you are a fit and experienced cyclist, it is suggested that you start no further east than the Middleton Top Visitor Centre, as there are two very steep sections.

ROUTE INFORMATION

National Routes: 68 (Tissington Trail), 54 (High Peak Trail)
Start: Tissington Trail: Station Road, Ashbourne, or the other side of the tunnel near Mapleton Road.
High Peak Trail: Middleton Top Visitor Centre.
Finish: Parsley Hay.
Distance: Tissington Trail: 13 miles (21km).
High Peak Trail: 11 miles (17.5km).

Grade: Easy, provided you walk the few hills on the High Peak Trail.
Surface: Dust surface.
Hills: Steady climb of almost 213m (700ft) from Ashbourne to Parsley Hay.

YOUNG & INEXPERIENCED CYCLISTS

Tissington Trail: Take care at the occasional road crossing. In Ashbourne, the old railway tunnel is lit, and if you start from Station Road

Ashbourne's pretty high street

on the south side of town, the journey will be traffic-free all the way and have easy gradients, apart from a fairly steep incline at Mapleton. **High Peak Trail:** There is a short, sharp incline at Hopton where you may need to walk. The route is traffic-free.

REFRESHMENTS
- Lots of choice in Ashbourne.

ASHBOURNE

- Dog and Partridge pub, Thorpe.
- Coffees and teas at Basset Wood Farm, Tissington.
- Waterloo Inn, Biggin.
- Dawn's Refreshments at Parsley Hay Cycle Centre.
- Cafe at Middleton Top.
- Cafe at National Stone Centre near Wirksworth.
- Rising Sun Inn, Middleton.

THINGS TO SEE & DO
- **Middleton Top Engine House:** built in 1829 to haul wagons up the Middleton incline. It's possible to see the engine in motion on selected dates between April and October; www.derbyshire.gov.uk
- **National Stone Centre on High Peak Trail, near Wirksworth:** a Site of Special Scientific Interest (SSSI), the centre contains six former quarries, four lime kilns and over 120 disused lead mine shafts, along with rocks, minerals and wildlife treasures; 01629 824833; www.nationalstonecentre.org.uk

Tissington village

TISSINGTON & HIGH PEAK TRAILS

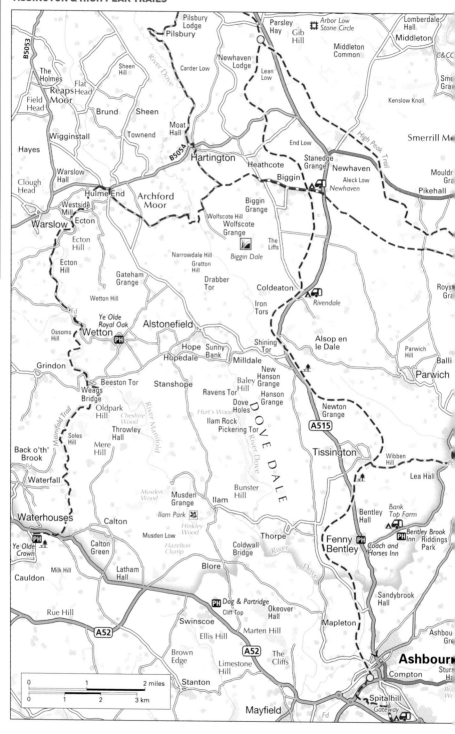

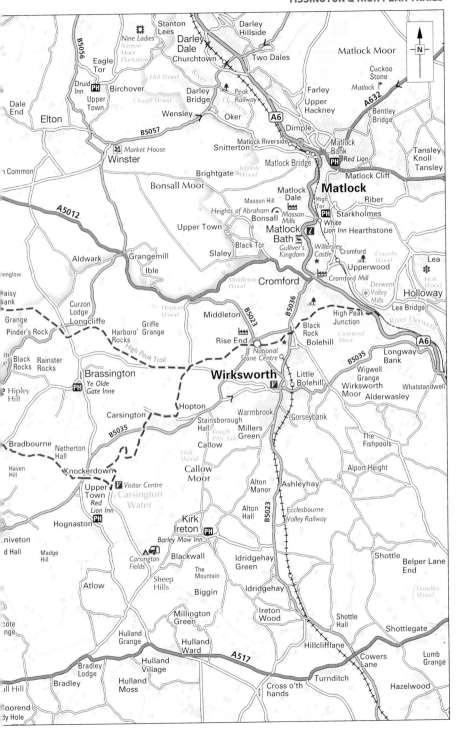

TRAIN STATIONS
Experienced riders only: Cromford;
Buxton; Derby.

BIKE HIRE
- Ashbourne Cycle Hire: 01335 343156
- Middleton Top Cycle Hire: 01629 823204
- Peak Cycle Hire, Parsley Hay: 01298 84493

FURTHER INFORMATION
- To view or print National Cycle Network
  routes, visit www.sustrans.org.uk
- Maps for this area are available to buy from
  www.sustransshop.co.uk
- Derbyshire Tourist Information:
  0800 0199 881; www.visitderbyshire.co.uk
- Ashbourne Tourist Information:
  01335 343666; www.visitpeakdistrict.com
- Tissington and High Peak Trails Information:
  www.derbyshire-peakdistrict.co.uk

ROUTE DESCRIPTION
Tissington Trail:
Start at Station Road in Ashbourne, then take
the traffic-free path through the Ashbourne
Tunnel. You then follow the railway path all the
way to Parsley Hay. There is a relatively steep
incline at Mapleton. En route, you'll pass near
Thorpe, one of the railway stopping points on
the original line, and Tissington – a perfect
village, with duckpond, picturesque cottages,
historic church and tearooms. The route
continues close to Alsop en le Dale and
Hartington station, just over a mile from
Hartington village, where you can see the old
signal box. The Tissington Trail meets the High
Peak Trail at Parsley Hay.

High Peak Trail:
Middleton Top is about 0.5 miles (0.8km)
northwest of Wirksworth. Shortly after starting
out, the trail bores through a hillside before
reaching the turn-off for Carsington Water and
Tissington (signed 54a – see below). The main
trail continues westwards, climbing the short,

sharp Hopton Incline – you may want to get
off here and walk. Next, watch out for the long,
curving stone-built causeway, where the path
turns through 90 degrees, just before
Longcliffe. Now you're in real White Peak
country, where the skilled masonry of the
original railway engineers blends wonderfully
with the surrounding homes, field walls and
rock faces. Dramatic long views alternate with
craggy cuttings along one of the most
spectacular cyclepaths in Britain until you
reach the relative enclosure of the tea-stop
at Parsley Hay.

As an alternative, there is a link on Route
54a that leaves High Peak Trail just north of
Hopton village and joins the Tissington Trail
at Tissington, taking in the visitor centre at
Carsington Water on the way. Much of
this runs on-lane, some is quite steep and
there are several busier road crossings,
so this section is better suited to more
experienced riders.

NEARBY CYCLE ROUTES
Tissington Trail forms part of the Pennine
Cycleway, Route 68 – a 350-mile (563km)
challenge route between Derby and Berwick-
upon-Tweed.

High Peak Trail is part of National Route 54,
which runs from Derby to Burton upon Trent,
Lichfield and Birmingham.

Route 6 goes from Derby to Nottingham in
one direction, and Loughborough and Leicester
in the other.

Other waymarked or traffic-free
rides include:
- Carsington Water, an 8-mile (13km)
  circular ride.
- Manifold Trail: Waterhouses to Hulme End
  (see page 98).
- Mickleover Trail, going from Derby
  to Hilton.
- Derby Canal Path and the Cloud Trail,
  Derby to Worthington (see page 82).

AROUND GRANTHAM

Discover this pretty corner of Lincolnshire, with its attractive honey-coloured stone villages, panoramic views across the vale of Belvoir and the tranquil Grantham Canal, teeming with wildlife.

For centuries, Grantham was the preferred stopping place for kings and noblemen travelling up and down the country. The Angel and Royal Hotel on the High Street was originally a court of King John, while the George Shopping Centre was a coaching inn, mentioned in Charles Dickens' *Nicholas Nickleby*.

This pleasant circular country ride takes you along quiet roads, canal towpaths and a disused railway. Grantham Canal once comprised 33 miles (53km) of water, joining Grantham to the River Trent at Nottingham. As you ride alongside it, it is worth looking out for swans, ducks, coots, moorhens, herons, even cormorants. Overall, this route is one to be enjoyed at a leisurely pace, and there are several opportunities to stop in the pretty villages along the way.

ROUTE INFORMATION

National Routes: 15, 64
Start and Finish: Grantham train station.
Distance: 23.5 miles (37.5km).
Grade: Easy.
Surface: Mainly smooth surfaces, stone paths and roads.
Hills: There is a short steep section from the Grantham Canal up to Harlaxton, another short steep uphill section just after Harlaxton, and one steep downhill section approaching Denton.

YOUNG & INEXPERIENCED CYCLISTS

With allowance for the hills and the length of the ride, all sections are suitable for everyone, as long as care is taken on the roads and by the canal.

REFRESHMENTS

- Lots of choice in Grantham.
- The Gregory pub, Harlaxton.
- The Welby Arms pub, Denton.
- The Chequers and Rutland Arms pubs, Woolsthorpe by Belvoir.

THINGS TO SEE & DO

- Grantham House: handsome town house, with architectural features from various eras

and riverside walled garden; 01476 564705; www.nationaltrust.org.uk
- Belton House, north of Grantham: 17th-century country house, with magnificent interiors, beautiful gardens and extensive parkland; 01476 566116; www.nationaltrust.org.uk
- Belvoir Castle: breathtaking views over the Vale of Belvoir; costumed guides show visitors impressive collections of period art and furniture; the grounds include a beautiful rose garden and a Victorian valley garden; 01476 871002; www.belvoircastle.com

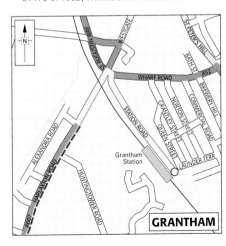

AROUND GRANTHAM

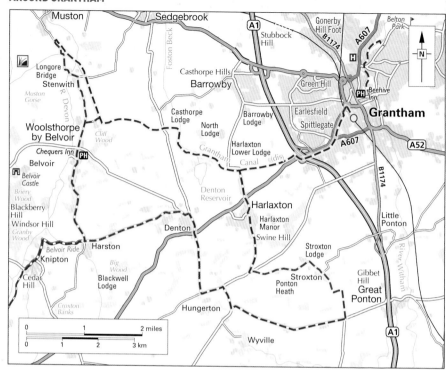

TRAIN STATIONS
Grantham.

BIKE HIRE
None locally.

FURTHER INFORMATION
- To view or print National Cycle Network routes, visit www.sustrans.org.uk
- Lincolnshire County Council's free leaflet *Grantham–Lincolnshire Cycle Routes* describes this route in detail. Map 5 in Lincolnshire County Council's free maps series covers the area around Grantham; 01522 782070
- Grantham Tourist Information: 01476 406166; www.grantham-online.co.uk
- Southwest Lincolnshire Tourist Information: 01476 406166; www.southwestlincs.com

ROUTE DESCRIPTION
From Grantham station, turn left down Station Road and left at the traffic lights into Harlaxton Road (A607). Follow the shared cycle/ pedestrian path for about a mile (1.6km). Just under the A1 flyover, carefully cross the road and follow the signs for National Route 15 down a narrow track to the canal. Carry on along the towpath to the second bridge and a National Cycle Network milepost. Leave the towpath, go up to the road, cross the canal and cycle uphill to the crossroads. Go carefully over the main road into Harlaxton village. At the shop, turn left into High Street and so to Swine Hill. Turn left at a T-junction, then turn right after about 100m (110 yards), at the sign for Stroxton.

After the village pond, go right into a gated road marked 'unsuitable for motors'. A little care is needed here, as the surface is loose and stony in places. The path turns left and then right before reaching a crossroads. Turn right, then right again at the junction. At the next T-junction, turn left, following signs for Croxton, then turn right on the road signposted to Denton. Carefully recross the main road and coast down the village street, following the

Belvoir Castle

Gentle offroad cycling

road as it bends left at a junction, then right. Turn left at the sign for Harston and Knipton; this road climbs very gently and crosses Sewerston Lane.

At Harston, turn right in the village (signed to Woolsthorpe) and go straight down through the crossroads at Woolsthorpe by Belvoir. Ignoring the turning on the right, continue to a T-junction, where you turn left at the sign for Stenwith. After the humpback bridge over the canal, the road bends left, then right. After 400m (439 yards), turn right through the large gap in the roadside woods – this is the access to Route 15 and Sedgebrook Mill (private).

Turn right again and enjoy a peaceful ride through the trees before dropping down to the Grantham Canal towpath and turning left. (To visit the Rutland Arms pub, turn right.) With the canal on your right, simply follow the route back to Grantham. Note that you will need a canal permit to cycle part of this route. This can be downloaded free at www.waterscape.com/cycling, or call 0845 671 5530.

NEARBY CYCLE ROUTES

National Route 15 carries on to Nottingham from Stenwith – not all of this is signed. It shares a section with Route 64, which continues to Newark-on-Trent and Lincoln.

Route 64 runs south from Woolsthorpe by Belvoir to Market Harborough, via Melton Mowbray (see page 62).

AROUND SOUTHWELL

Southwell has many elegant Regency houses but its architectural jewel is the Minster Church, which boasts some of the finest medieval stone carving in England. Just outside the town is the Workhouse, a 19th-century institution restored by the National Trust, where you can find out what life was really like for Victorian paupers in this starkly atmospheric building.

The Southwell Trail is a disused railway track that has been redeveloped to include a nature reserve and a traffic-free route for walkers, cyclists and horse-riders. This route uses the trail from Southwell to Bilsthorpe and then enters Sherwood Pines Forest Park. Sherwood Pines offers a variety of signed routes, providing a network of riding possibilities for all ages and abilities.

ROUTE INFORMATION
National Route: 6
Start and Finish: Car park, Station Road, Southwell.
Distance: 25 miles (40km).
Grade: Medium.
Surface: Mainly stone disused railway and forest tracks, which can be uneven in places, especially in the forest.
Hills: The Southwell Trail from Southwell to Bilsthorpe is just under 7 miles (11km) of gentle ascent.

YOUNG & INEXPERIENCED CYCLISTS
Most of this route is traffic-free but the stone surfacing can be tiring to ride on.

REFRESHMENTS
- Lots of choice in Southwell.
- The Red Lion and Plough Inn pubs, Farnsfield.
- The Copper Beech and Stanton Arms pubs, Bilsthorpe.
- Cafe at Sherwood Pines Forest Park.

THINGS TO SEE & DO
- **Southwell Minster:** magnificent 12th-century minster with twin 'pepper pot' spires; 01636 812649; www.southwellminster.org
- **The Workhouse:** well-preserved and atmospheric 19th-century workhouse; 01636 817260; www.nationaltrust.org.uk
- **Southwell Trail Local Nature Reserve:** supports a wide range of habitats, including acid grassland and species-rich meadows and woodlands; 08449 808080; www.nottinghamshire.gov.uk
- **Sherwood Pines Forest Park:** 3,300 acres of waymarked walking trails, several play areas, visitor centre and Go Ape!, a high-wire forest adventure; 0845 367 3787; www.forestry.gov.uk; www.goape.co.uk

TRAIN STATIONS
Fiskerton.

Southwell Minster and entrance arch

Inside Southwell Minster

BIKE HIRE

- Sherwood Pines Cycles: 01623 822855;
  www.sherwoodpinescycles.co.uk

FURTHER INFORMATION

- To view or print National Cycle Network
  routes, visit www.sustrans.org.uk
- Map no. 3 (*Cycling in Newark and Sherwood*) in Nottinghamshire County Council's free *Cycling in Nottinghamshire* series of maps; 0115 977 4585
- Southwell Tourist Information:
  01636 819038;
  www.newark-sherwooddc.gov.uk
- Newark and Sherwood Tourist Information:
  01636 650000;
  www.newark-sherwooddc.gov.uk
- Mountain Bike Trails, Sherwood Pines Map: 01623 822447; email: enquiries.sherwood@forestry.gsi.gov.uk

Sherwood Forest

ROUTE DESCRIPTION

This is a 'lollipop' ride, meaning that it is part circular and part there-and-back.

Join the traffic-free path at the back of the car park at Station Road, Southwell, and follow the Southwell Trail to Bilsthorpe. At just less than 7 miles (11km) long, the Trail is a constant but gentle ascent for pretty much its entire length. It is an old railway track and the surface has not been tarmacked. After 4 miles (6.5km), the path splits and the left fork will take you to Farnsfield (for pubs and shops) but you should follow the right-hand branch to Bilsthorpe, passing under the A617. In Bilsthorpe, cycle on Forest Link until you reach a roundabout, where you turn left onto Eakring Road. Cycle through the village and, after 1 mile (1.6km), turn left at the T-junction onto Deerdale Road. Cross carefully over the A614 and within a mile you reach Sherwood Pines Forest Park. Here, there are many choices of cycle routes on forest tracks. For the visitor centre and cafe, turn right in the forest and follow the large blue posts that waymark the route. Turn right onto the green waymarked route when there is that choice and pass the visitor centre on your left.

For the return trip, either go back the way you came or continue on the green waymarked route until you can turn right onto the blue route. Continue on the blue route until it joins National Route 6 and turn left. Follow signed Route 6 through the forest. After the level crossing, turn left (east) onto another forest track, which becomes a road leading to the A614. Cross over and follow Mickledale Lane into Bilsthorpe. At the T-junction, turn right onto Eakring Road. At the roundabout, turn right onto Forest Link, leading to the Southwell Trail and a downhill ride back to Southwell.

NEARBY CYCLE ROUTES

National Route 6 links Sherwood Forest northwards to Worksop and on to Rotherham and Sheffield. Going south, it passes through Nottingham, Beeston, Long Eaton and Derby.

Route 64, from Market Harborough to Lincoln via Melton Mowbray and Newark-on-Trent, includes a traffic-free railway path.

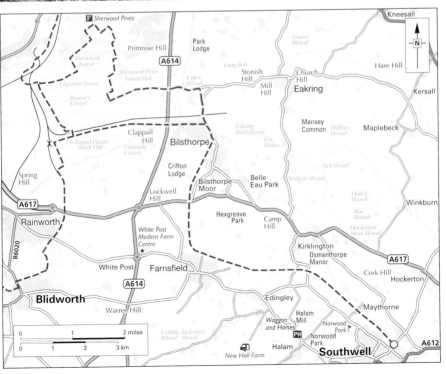

LINCOLN TO HARBY CIRCUIT

Lincoln is dominated by its 11th-century cathedral and castle. The castle, on the site of a Roman fortress and settlement, was built as an invulnerable stronghold on a hilltop 61m (200ft) above the River Witham.

This ride is a circular route that starts and finishes by Brayford Pool in Lincoln and runs westwards along the Roman Fossdyke Canal. It uses a dismantled railway alongside Old Wood in Skellingthorpe to reach Harby. One of the most significant events in Harby's history happened in 1290 when Queen Eleanor, Queen Consort of Edward I, died there of a 'slow fever' – the story is recounted on an information board near the church. She was commemorated by the king with 12 memorial 'Eleanor crosses' between Lincoln and London, including one at Charing Cross in London.

The return trip takes in Whisby, Thorpe on the Hill and North Hykeham before using the traffic-free Riverside Path back into Lincoln.

Cyclists seen from Harby Bridge

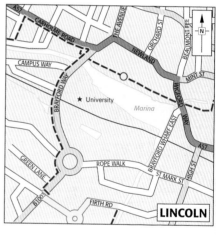

ROUTE INFORMATION
National Route: 64
Regional Route: 93
Start and Finish: Cinema, Brayford Wharf North, Lincoln.
Distance: 20 miles (32km).
Grade: Easy.

Surface: Smooth-surfaced paths.
Hills: Gentle.

YOUNG & INEXPERIENCED CYCLISTS
The route uses long lengths of traffic-free paths and quiet lanes. There are pavements beside the on-road sections in Lincoln and Hykeham for those who prefer to walk.

REFRESHMENTS
- Lots of choice in Lincoln.
- Pyewipe Inn, Fossdyke Canal.
- The Stone Arms and Plough pubs, Skellingthorpe.

River Witham, Lincoln

- The Bottle & Glass pub, Harby.
- The Struggler pub, Eagle.
- Cafe at Whisby Natural World, Whisby.

THINGS TO SEE & DO

- Lincoln Castle: one of the finest remaining Norman castles in England; holds one of only four original copies of the Magna Carta; 01522 511068; www.visitlincolnshire.com
- Lincoln Cathedral: one of the most superb Gothic buildings in Europe, with a rich and varied history; 01522 561600; www.lincolncathedral.com
- Steep Hill and Bailgate: historical areas of

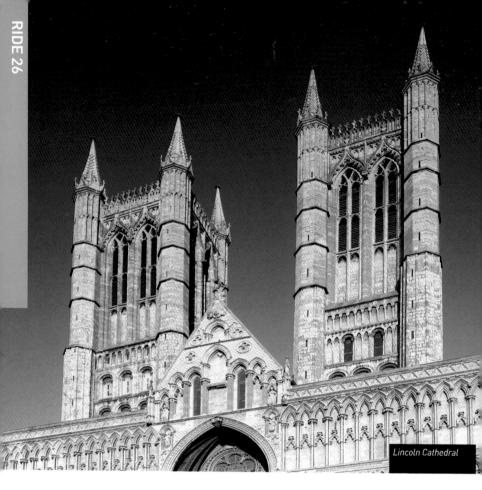

Lincoln Cathedral

Lincoln, crammed with specialist shops.
- **Old Wood, Skellingthorpe:** mixture of ancient oak, lime woodland and conifers; 01476 581111; www.woodlandtrust.org.uk
- **Whisby Nature Park:** flooded gravel pits surrounded by areas of lowland heath, grassland and woodland; 01507 526667; www.lincstrust.org.uk
- **Whisby Natural World:** state-of-the-art exhibitions, shop, cafe and stunning views; 01522 688868; www.naturalworldcentre.co.uk

TRAIN STATIONS
Lincoln Central; Hykeham.

BIKE HIRE
- Barnes Cycles, Newport, Lincoln: 01522 519813; www.barnescycles.co.uk

FURTHER INFORMATION
- To view or print National Cycle Network routes, visit www.sustrans.org.uk
- Lincolnshire County Council's free leaflet *Lincoln–Lincolnshire Cycle Routes* describes this route in detail. Map 3 in Lincolnshire County Council's free cycling map series covers the area around Lincoln; 01522 782070
- **Lincolnshire Tourist Information:** 01522 873256; www.visitlincolnshire.com

ROUTE DESCRIPTION
From the cinema at Brayford Wharf North, with Brayford Pool on your left, cycle along the traffic-free, signed route towards Whisby

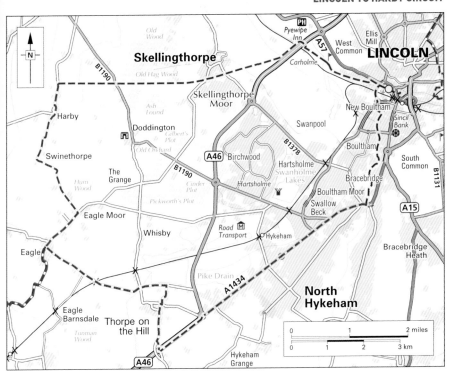

and Newark – this is National Route 64. Continue beside the Fossdyke Canal until you reach the Pyewipe Inn. Cross the car park and follow the road under the A46 and turn left, ramping up to a narrow bridge over the Fossdyke and railway. Follow the path for 4 miles (6.5km) through Skellingthorpe to the edge of Harby village. Turn left off the old railway line and, at the top of the ramp, turn right along Station Road. In Harby, turn left past the pub and left along Church Road, signed to Eagle. At the crossroads at Eagle Moor, turn right.

In Eagle, turn left to join Regional Route 93 and at the crossroads continue straight on to Whisby Nature Park. (Cycling is not allowed in the park itself.) Turn right opposite Whisby Nature Park and cycle up to Thorpe on the Hill, where you turn right and immediately left. As you pass the church, go straight on. Cross the A46 on a bridge and turn left. Just before the dual carriageway, turn right onto a path beside the A46 towards Lincoln. As you reach the

built-up area, cross the road and use the dedicated cycle lanes through North Hykeham. After 3 miles (5km), turn left through the car park of the Plough pub (signed City Centre) to get on the traffic-free Riverside Path. After 2 miles (3km), just before the retail park, turn left onto Firth Road, and at the small roundabout turn right. Cross Tritton Road using the cyclists' crossing facilities and turn right onto the cycle path, which takes you up and over the Fossdyke and the railway. Turn right after this flyover to return to Brayford Wharf North.

NEARBY CYCLE ROUTES
National Route 64 continues through Newark into Notts. The main route through Lincolnshire is Route 1, known as the Hull to Harwich cycle route, passing through Boston, Lincoln and Market Rasen. The main traffic-free section of this route is the Water Rail Way (see page 118), following the River Witham between Lincoln, Bardney and Kirkstead Bridge (near Woodhall Spa), and between Langrick Bridge and Boston.

THE WATER RAIL WAY

The main traffic-free section of the route along the former Lincoln to Boston railway line follows the River Witham from Lincoln, past Washingborough, to Bardney and on to Southrey, Stixwould and Kirkstead Bridge, close to the town of Woodhall Spa. The path features vast open fenland landscapes, with long views and expansive skies. To the north stands Lincoln Cathedral, to the south St Botolph's Church (the 'Stump'), which, on a clear day, can be seen from many miles away.

Many of the artworks commissioned for the sculpture trail along the route were inspired by the poems of Alfred, Lord Tennyson, and commemorate the 200th anniversary of his birth in Lincolnshire in 1809. Cyclists can learn about the history surrounding the trail and the wildlife it attracts from the information boards along the route, as well as enjoying the sculptures *Lincoln Red Cattle* and *Lincoln Longwool Sheep* created by artist Sally Matthews, and *Lincolnshire Curly Coat Pigs* by Nigel Sardeson, all inspired by the local environment and breeds of animal.

The spectacular triple-towered Norman and Gothic cathedral in Lincoln stands on a limestone plateau among the medieval buildings of the old city and can be seen from the Water Rail Way as far south as Stixwould.

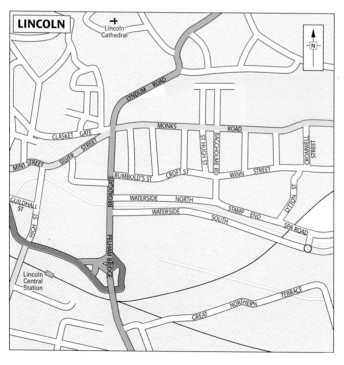

ROUTE INFORMATION

National Route: 1
Start: Waterside South Bridge, Lincoln.
Finish: Kirkstead Bridge, near Woodhall Spa.
Distance: 15 miles (24km). Shorter options: from Lincoln to Bardney 9 miles (14.5km); Bardney to Woodhall Spa 7 miles (11km).
Grade: Easy.
Surface: The bridleway section southeast of Bardney can be muddy when wet. The surface on the rest of the route is a good hard surface and easily accessible in all weathers.
Hills: None.

'Lincoln Red Cattle' by Sally Matthews

YOUNG & INEXPERIENCED CYCLISTS

This route is flat and almost entirely traffic-free. At Kirkstead Bridge, you can walk along the pavement on the road bridge.

REFRESHMENTS

- Lots of choice in Lincoln.
- Carpenter's Arms pub just off the route in Fiskerton (cross the river at Five Mile Bridge).
- Cafe at the Goods Shed, Bardney.
- Pubs in Washingborough, Bardney, Southrey and at Kirkstead Bridge and Martin Dales.
- Lots of choice in Woodhall Spa.

THINGS TO SEE & DO

- Lincoln Cathedral: mostly 13th century with some parts dating back to 1072; 01522 561600; www.lincolncathedral.com
- Lincoln Castle: dating from 1068, the castle was used as a court and prison for 900 years; 01522 511068; www.visitlincolnshire.com
- Ellis Windmill, Lincoln: dating from 1798 and working until the 1940s; 01522 528448; www.lincolnshire.gov.uk
- Fiskerton Fen Nature Reserve: 01507 526667; www.lincstrust.org.uk
- Bardney Abbey, just off the route in Bardney: www.lincsheritage.org
- Bardney Heritage Centre: 01526 397299;

www.lincsheritageforum.org.uk
- Kirkstead Abbey, just off the route near Kirkstead Bridge: abbey ruins dating from 1139; www.woodhallspa.org

Woodhall Spa:
- Cottage Museum: reflecting the history of the town; 01526 353775; www.woodhallspa.org
- Kinema in the Woods: Britain's only rear-projection cinema, opened in 1922; 01526 352166; www.thekinemainthewoods.co.uk
- Moor Farm and Kirkby Moor Nature Reserves: heath and woodland near Woodhall Spa; www.lincstrust.org.uk

TRAIN STATIONS

Lincoln Central.

BIKE HIRE

- Bardney Heritage Centre: 01526 397299
- Barnes Cycles, Newport, Lincoln; 01522 519813; www.barnescycles.co.uk

FURTHER INFORMATION

- To view or print National Cycle Network routes, visit www.sustrans.org.uk
- Maps 3 and 4 in Lincolnshire County Council's free cycling maps series cover this ride; 01522 782070

'Seal' by Steve Elderkin

'Boston Pendulum' by Paul Robbrecht

- Lincolnshire Tourist Information:
  01522 782332; www.visitlincolnshire.com
- Woodhall Spa Tourist Information:
  01526 353775; www.woodhallspa.org
- Water Rail art and route leaflets are available
  from 01522 782070 www.visitlincolnshire.
  com/things-to-do/outdoors/waterways/
  walking-and-cycling

ROUTE DESCRIPTION

From Witham Park at the east end of Waterside South in Lincoln, take the Water Rail Way path along the south side of the River Witham towards Washingborough. The route follows a tree-lined strip of land between the river and the Sincil Drain, to pass Five Mile Bridge (cross here for Fiskerton) and along to Bardney Lock. In Bardney, choose the traffic-free summer route, which may be muddy after rain, or the all-weather route on roads through the village

and out along the B1190, then through Southrey to join the path again just after the village.

The Water Rail Way then follows the east side of the river to Kirkstead Bridge, where you can take roads into Woodhall Spa or cross over the bridge to Martin Dales. All along the route you will see wonderful sculptures.

For a longer ride, continue on the Water Rail Way on minor roads to Langrick Bridge, then on a traffic-free section, again following the River Witham, into Boston (17 miles/27.5km).

NEARBY CYCLE ROUTES

From Woodhall Spa, the Water Rail Way follows National Route 1 on minor roads to Langrick Bridge, then a further traffic-free section by the River Witham into Boston. From Boston, Route 1 follows quiet roads into Cambridgeshire. Lincoln is a hub on the National Cycle Network, with both Routes 1 and 64 meeting in the city centre. Route 64 follows a traffic-free path west along the Roman Fossdyke Canal before joining the railway path to Skellingthorpe and Harby (see page 114).

Quiet lanes link the route to a short section of traffic-free path at Collingham and under busy main roads into Newark, where a further 5 miles (8km) of traffic-free path run south from Newark Northgate station to Cotham.

'Curly Coat Pigs' by Nigel Sardeson

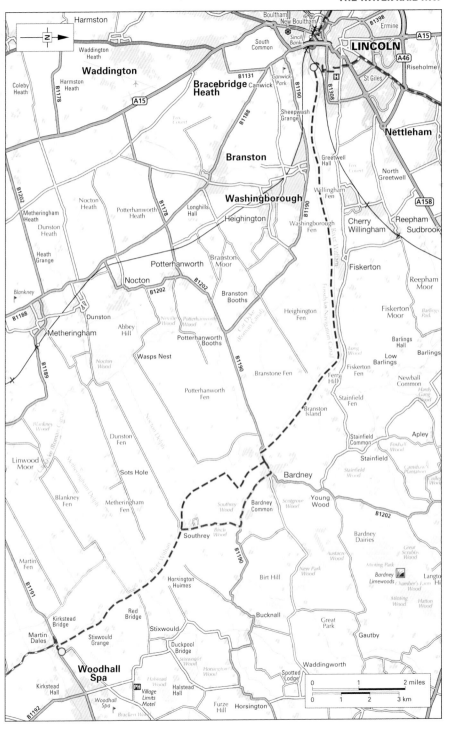

WOODHALL SPA

Set amid magnificent pine woods, Woodhall Spa is an Edwardian inland resort with real character. The town would not have existed without the vision of John Parkinson. In the early 1800s, his dream was to open a coal mine, plant a forest and build a new town. The discovery of spa water was the turning point and he set about building 'a town without streets'. Broad tree-lined avenues and large residential plots were created, and that same policy is maintained to this day, giving the town a genuine feeling of space.

Part of this circular ride follows the Water Rail Way, named after the secretive water rail bird, which has been seen from the path. The 33-mile (53km) Water Rail Way includes 20 miles (32km) of traffic-free path along the former Lincoln to Boston railway line beside the River Witham. The Water Rail Way boasts an extensive series of artworks based on Lincolnshire themes, animals past and present, and sculptures inspired by the poetry of Alfred, Lord Tennyson, who was born in the county.

The Pinewoods, Woodhall Spa

ROUTE INFORMATION
National Route: 1
Start and Finish: Royal Square Gardens (junction of Station Road and Tattershall Road), centre of Woodhall Spa.
Distance: 16 miles (25.5km).
Grade: Easy.
Surface: Tarmac.
Hills: None.

YOUNG & INEXPERIENCED CYCLISTS

The route uses quiet roads and a section of the Water Rail Way, a peaceful traffic-free path. The start of the ride in the centre of Woodhall Spa follows a busier road but there are pavements if young and inexperienced cyclists prefer to walk this section.

REFRESHMENTS
- Cafes/tearooms and pubs in Woodhall Spa.
- The Ebrington Arms pub, Kirkby on Bain.
- The Railway Hotel pub, Kirkstead Bridge.

THINGS TO SEE & DO
- Cottage Museum, Woodhall Spa: award-winning museum, with an excellent display of local photographs and memorabilia; tourist information provided in summer; 01526 353775; www.woodhallspa.org
- Dambusters Memorial, Royal Gardens,

Peaceful scenes along the pathway

If you're lucky you may spot a water rail

Woodhall Spa: erected in 1987 to serve the memory of the World War II heroes of 617 Squadron; 01526 353775; www.woodhallspa.org

- Pinewoods: mature oak, Scots pine, beech and a lot of regenerating birch; favoured by wildlife, including a notable range of woodland birds such as great spotted woodpeckers; 01476 581111; www.woodlandtrust.org.uk

- Kinema in the Woods, Woodhall Spa: housed in a converted cricket pavilion, this is the only rear-projection cinema still regularly showing films in Britain; 01526 352166;

WOODHALL SPA

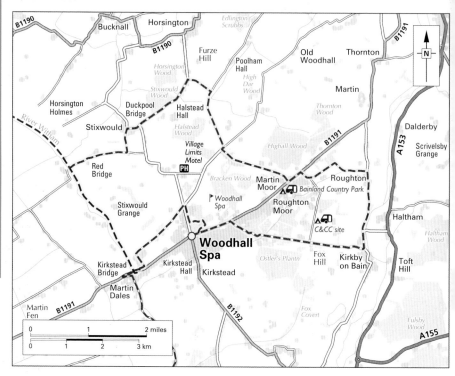

www.thekinemainthewoods.co.uk
- **Roughton Moor Wood:** former heathland; fine trees, interesting fungi and varied bird population; 01507 526667; www.lincstrust.org.uk
- **Kirby Moor Nature Reserve:** diverse habitat, with a wide range of plants and animals; 01507 526667; www.lincstrust.org.uk
- **Kirkstead Abbey:** ruins of one of the medieval abbeys built in the Witham Valley and founded in 1139; 01526 353775; www.woodhallspa.org

TRAIN STATIONS
Metheringham; Lincoln Central.

BIKE HIRE
- Bardney Heritage Centre, Bardney: 01526 397299

FURTHER INFORMATION
- To view or print National Cycle Network routes, visit www.sustrans.org.uk

- Lincolnshire County Council's free leaflet *Woodhall Spa–Lincolnshire Cycle Routes* and Map 4 in Lincolnshire County Council's free cycling map series cover this area; 01522 782070
- **Woodhall Spa Tourist Information (summer only):** 01526 353775; www.woodhallspa.org
- Water Rail art and route leaflets are available from 01522 782070; www.visitlincolnshire. com/things-to-do/outdoors/waterways/walking-and-cycling

ROUTE DESCRIPTION
Leave the Royal Square Gardens and cycle through Woodhall Spa along Station Road (the Broadway), past the Golf Hotel and the National Golf Centre, to Kirkby Lane. Turn right (signed Kirkby on Bain) and enjoy the Roughton Moor Wood and Ostler's Plantation. At the T-junction, turn left towards Roughton. In Roughton, turn left and left again onto the Broadway (both signed Woodhall Spa). Take care and turn first right into Sandy Lane

'Lincoln Red Cattle' by
Sally Matthews

Bardney Viaduct

(signed Horsington). At the T-junction by the
Wellington Monument, dogleg right and then
left (signed Poolham). After a mile (1.6km),
turn left into Ings Lane (signposted Stixwould).
At the T-junction, turn left (signed Stixwould),
past Stixwould Wood. In Stixwould, turn right
(signed Bucknall) and then left into Station
Road. At the tiny T-junction, turn right and
continue straight on until you reach the former
Stixwould station. Turn left through the car
park and join the Water Rail Way (National
Route 1). Look out for the sculpture by Sally
Matthews, take a rest on one of the many seats
and enjoy views of the river and across the
fields to Woodhall Spa.

Take the path to Kirkstead Bridge and,
following the signs, leave the old railway line at
the former station house at Woodhall Junction.

Follow Witham Road to the T-junction with
Station Road, turn right, then left along Mill
Lane. At the crossroads, turn right (signed
Woodhall Spa) and then left into Coronation
Road (signed Kinema in the Woods). Turn right
along King George Avenue and, at the
T-junction, turn right into Spa Road and right
again to Station Road, to return to the Royal
Square Gardens.

NEARBY CYCLE ROUTES

This route follows a short section of the Water
Rail Way, part of National Route 1, which can be
followed south to Boston and the fens or north
to Lincoln (see page 118) and on to Hull.

NEXT STEPS...

We hope you have enjoyed the cycle rides in this book.

Sustrans developed the National Cycle Network to act as a catalyst for bringing cycling (and walking) back into our everyday lives. Between the 1950s and the mid-1970s cycling in the UK fell by 80%. Cycling now accounts for only about 2% of all journeys made in the UK, a fraction of what we used to achieve.

When you consider that nearly 6 in 10 car journeys are under 5 miles, it makes you wonder what the potential for increasing levels of cycling is. Evidence shows that, for local journeys under 5 miles, most of us could make 9 out of 10 journeys on foot, bike or public transport if there was more investment in making it possible to leave the car behind.

And why not? We can all be more savvy when it comes to travel. One small step becomes one giant leap if we all start walking away from less healthy lifestyles and pedalling our way towards happier children and a low carbon world.

And that's where Sustrans comes in. Sustainable travel means carbon-reducing, energy-efficient, calorie-burning, money-saving travel. Here are a few things that we think make sense. If you agree, join us.

- Snail's pace – 20mph or less on our streets where we live, go to school, shop and work – make it the norm, not just when there's snow or ice on the roads.

- Closer encounters – planning that focuses on good non-motorised access, so that we can reach more post offices, schools, shops, doctors and dentists without the car.

- People spaces – streets where kids can play hopscotch or football and be free-range, and where neighbours can meet and chat, and safe, local walking and cycling routes, to school and beyond.

- Road revolution – build miles and miles of bike paths that don't evaporate when they meet a road.

- Find our feet – campaign for pedestrian-friendly city centres, or wide boulevards with regular pedestrian crossings and slow-moving traffic.

- Better buses – used by millions, under-invested by billions and, if affordable, reliable and pleasant to use, could make local car journeys redundant.

- More car clubs – a car club on every street corner and several for every new-build estate.

- Rewards for car-sharing – get four in a car and take more than half the cars off the road.

- Trains – more of them, and cheaper.

- Become a staycationer – and holiday at home. Mountains, beaches, culture, great beer, good food and a National Cycle Network that connects them all.

If we work towards these goals we have a chance of delivering our fair share of the 80% reduction in CO_2 by mid-century that we're now committed to by law, and some of the 100% reduction that many climate experts now consider essential.

To find out more and join the movement, visit www.sustrans.org.uk

Free. Clean. Green.

Photo: Rita Platts/ Sustrans

Few people would say that they don't care about the environment, don't want to get fit or don't care about the damage pollution is doing to local communities – but what's the answer? The humble bike: a great way to get from A to B, cut carbon emissions and get fit at the same time. The bike is the greenest machine on the road, and Sustrans is doing everything it can to help people cycle more. Sustrans developed the National Cycle Network to help bring cycling (and walking) back into everyday life.

Cycling only accounts for 2% of all the journeys made in the UK today. 90% of all journeys under five miles could be made by foot, public transport or bike. And we are trying to do everything possible to make this happen. Help us provide everyone with a greener way to travel.

If you care about the environment and love cycling, you should support Sustrans. Get online at sustrans.org.uk, join the movement and find out how Sustrans can improve your cycling experience.

sustrans

JOIN THE MOVEMENT

ACKNOWLEDGEMENTS

Vincent Cassar would like to thank Sustrans workers and rangers for their help and advice with the writing of this guide; especially Clyde Hinton, Robert Gullen, Mike Clarke, Alan White, Mike Thomas, John Cooke, Mike Cooper, Keith Drury, John Dyson, John Hallwood, David Martin, Geoff Shinner and John Woodward.

The Automobile Association would like to thank the following photographers, companies and picture libraries for their assistance in the preparation of this book.

Abbreviations for the picture credits are as follows – (t) top; (b) bottom; (l) left; (r) right; (c) centre; (dps) double page spread; (AA) AA World Travel Library

Front Cover: Thor's Cave, Manifold Valley, Staffordshire; AA/Tom Mackie.
Back cover: Dave Gorman; Pete Dadds/Avalon

3l J Bewley/Sustrans; 3r AA/C Jones; 4 Pete Dadds/Avalon; 5 Courtesy Sustrans, all rights reserved; 6/7 AA/Caroline Jones; 7t David Martin/Sustrans; 7c AA/M Hayward; 7b AA/AA; 11tl Jon Bewley/Sustrans; 11tr Jon Bewley/Sustrans; 11c Jon Bewley/Sustrans; 11bc Andy Huntley/Sustrans; 11br Pru Comben/Sustrans; 13t Jon Bewley/Sustrans; 13c Nicola Jones/Sustrans; 13b Jon Bewley/Sustrans; 14 AA/C Jones; 15 AA/M Moody; 17l AA/M Moody; 17r J Bewley/Sustrans; 19tr AA/Michael Moody; 21 Colin Underhill/Alamy; 22 Courtesy Sustrans; 23t AA/M Short; 23b AA/C Nicholls; 24 Colin Underhill/Alamy; 26/27 AA/M Hayward; 29 AA/R Surman; 30/31 AA/A Tryner; 33 Simon Whaley/Alamy; 35t AA/J Wyand; 35c The National Trust Photolibrary/Alamy; 37t AA/C Jones; 37c John Grimshaw/Sustrans; 38/39 AA/J Welsh; 40 The National Trust Photolibrary/Alamy; 42/43b Colin Underhill/Alamy; 43tr Courtesy Edward Healy/

Sustrans; 44t David McGill/Photoshot; 46 Courtesy Sustrans, all rights reserved; 47 AA/M Birkitt; 48t AA/P Baker; 48b Perminder Balou/Sustrans; 49 Courtesy Sustrans, all rights reserved; 50/51 AA/M Birkitt; 53t Gary Moseley/Alamy; 53b AA/M Birkitt; 54 J Bewley/Sustrans; 55 AA/M Birkitt; 56 J Bewley/Sustrans; 58/59 AA/M Birkitt; 61t Robert Bird/Alamy; 61c AA/M Birkitt; 63t AA/T Wyles; 63c AA/P Baker; 65 Charles Bowman/Alamy; 67 AA/P Baker; 69t Graham Oliver/Alamy; 69c John Palmer/Sustrans; 71 AA/J Welsh; 73t AA/J Wyand; 73c Robin Weaver/Alamy; 74/75 Graham Oliver/Alamy; 77t Colin Underhill/Alamy; 77b Travel and Places/Alamy; 78/79 AA/AA; 80 Graham Oliver/Alamy; 81 AA/P Grogan; 83t Patrick Davis/Sustrans; 82/83 Robin Weaver/Alamy; 85 M-dash/Alamy; 86/87 WilliamRobinson/Alamy; 89t AA/J Mottershaw; 89b AA/M Moody ; 90/91 kris Mercer/Alamy; 91t AA/P Baker; 92 kris Mercer/Alamy; 94 The National Trust Photolibrary/Alamy; 95 The National Trust Photolibrary/Alamy; 96/97 AA/N Coates; 98/99 AA/T Mackie; 99t AA/T Mackie; 101 AA/T Mackie; 102 AA/T Mackie; 103 AA/T Mackie; 109t Tracey Foster/Alamy; 109c David Martin/Sustrans; 110 WebbTravel/Alamy; 111 Steve Taylor ARPS/Alamy; 112/113 David Mark/Alamy; 114 Paul Rea/Sustrans; 115 Tommy (Louth)/Alamy; 116 AA/T Mackie; 119 David Martin/Sustrans; 120tl David Martin/Sustrans ; 120tr David Martin/Sustrans; 120c David Martin/Sustrans ; 122 Robin Weaver/Alamy; 123t Courtesy Sustrans; 123c Andy Sands/naturepl.com; 125t David Martin/Sustrans; 125c David Martin/Sustrans.

Every effort has been made to trace the copyright holders, and we apologise in advance for any unintentional omissions or errors. We would be pleased to apply any corrections in the following edition of this publication.